THE SAMUEL AND ALTHEA STROUM LECTURES

IN JEWISH STUDIES

THE SAMUEL AND ALTHEA STROUM

The Yiddish Art Song
performed by Leon Lishner, basso, and Lazar Weiner, piano
(stereophonic record album)

The Holocaust in Historical Perspective
Yehuda Bauer

Zakhor: Jewish History and Jewish Memory
Yosef Hayim Yerushalmi

Jewish Mysticism and Jewish Ethics
Joseph Dan

The Invention of Hebrew Prose:
Modern Fiction and the Language of Realism
Robert Alter

Recent Archaeological Discoveries and Biblical Research
William G. Dever

Jewish Identity in the Modern World
Michael A. Meyer

I. L. Peretz and the Making
of Modern Jewish Culture
Ruth R. Wisse

LECTURES IN JEWISH STUDIES

STUDYING
theJEWISH
FUTURE

Calvin Goldscheider

UNIVERSITY OF WASHINGTON PRESS

Seattle and London

University of Washington Press
PO Box 50096, Seattle, WA 98145
www.washington.edu/uwpress

Library of Congress Cataloging-in-Publication Data
Goldscheider, Calvin.
Studying the Jewish future / Calvin Goldscheider.
p. cm.—(The Samuel and Althea Stroum lectures in Jewish studies)
A study of Jewish communities in the United States, Europe, and Israel.
Includes bibliographical references and index.
ISBN 0-295-98388-4 (cloth : alk. paper)
ISBN 0-295-98389-2 (paper : alk. paper)
1. Jews—Identity.
2. Jews—Social conditions—21st century.
3. Twenty-first century—Forecasts.
4. Population forecasting.
5. Social prediction.
6. Judaism—Social aspects.
I. Title. II. Series.
DS143.G614 2004   305.892'4—dc22   2004040713

THE SAMUEL AND ALTHEA STROUM LECTURES
IN JEWISH STUDIES

Samuel Stroum, businessman, community leader, and philanthropist, by a major gift to the Jewish Federation of Greater Seattle, established the Samuel and Althea Stroum Philanthropic Fund.

In recognition of Mr. and Mrs. Stroum's deep interest in Jewish history and culture, the Board of Directors of the Jewish Federation of Greater Seattle, in cooperation with the Jewish Studies Program of the Henry M. Jackson School of International Studies at the University of Washington, established an annual lectureship at the University of Washington known as the Samuel and Althea Stroum Lectureship in Jewish Studies. This lectureship makes it possible to bring to the area outstanding scholars and interpreters of Jewish thought, thus promoting a deeper understanding of Jewish history, religion, and culture. Such understanding can lead to an enhanced appreciation of the Jewish contributions to the historical and cultural traditions that have shaped the American nation.

The terms of the gift also provide for the publication from time to time of the lectures or other appropriate materials resulting from or related to the lectures.

To Minnie Goldscheider,

mother, grandmother, and great-grandmother,

another typical extraordinary Jew.

May she continue to be inspired

by her memories of the past

and by future dreams of her expanding family.

CONTENTS

PREFACE

The essays in this book were originally prepared as lectures in the Stroum series at the University of Washington. The occasion provided me the opportunity to systematically rethink and reassess the comparative features of contemporary Jewish communities in Europe, Israel, and the United States. In the book, as in the lectures, I focus on issues of the future as a framework for understanding the past and for interpreting contemporary Jewish communities. I study the future not in order to predict what will be, but in order to read the ways in which others have projected or envisioned the future. I attempt to disentangle the theoretical, ideological, and empirical bases of forecasts because conceptions of the future inform much of our readings of history and contemporary Jewish life. This approach offers a new and different perspective from which to examine contemporary Jewish communities and modern Jewish history.

The lectures themselves were delivered to a large and diverse audience of scholars, students, Jewish communal leaders, and community activists in the Seattle metropolitan area. I therefore kept the technical parts of the lectures to a bare minimum. Extensive public discussions followed the three lectures that make up the core of chapters 2, 4, 5, and 6. I substantially revised and extended these lectures as I converted them into essays, both because I learned much from the subsequent discussions and because there are fundamental differences between oral and written presentations.

An abbreviated version of chapter 3 was presented to a small group of interested faculty at the University of Washington. I had prepared a more technical and detailed seminar but did not present it, because the faculty members who appeared were largely from the humanities and not, as I had expected, from the University of Washington's Center for Studies in Demography and Ecology. I therefore spontaneously revised the prepared talk to address more general issues of population projections. It was a valuable experience for me, and I decided that the resulting lecture was of sufficient interest to fit the character of the book as a whole. Chapter 3 is a revision, integrating the materials I presented and the original lecture I had prepared.

I often use the personal voice in these essays. That has not been my style for most of my scholarly writing. But over the years, my several co-authors and editors (as well as the grammar software on my computer) have chided me for using the passive voice, so I have finally learned to use the first person singular. I use it here as a transition from the lectures I gave in the Stroum series and also because my discovery of how to study the future should be understood as personal. The materials I present here are my interpretations of the evidence and my assessments of and conclusions about the available research. I believe the interpretation I offer is based on the total array of evidence available at the beginning of the twenty-first century. I know from discussions, disagreements, and public debates with colleagues and friends that mine is often not the most currently acceptable set of explanations. I set forth in the chapters that follow the limitations of alternative perspectives and interpretations. Others, in reviewing this book, will not hesitate to point out the limitations of my own interpretations.

In the process of revising these lectures for publication, I used several occasions to obtain the reactions of colleagues and general audiences. One of the most important forums, and the most recent, was the meeting of the Association of Jewish Studies in December 2001. I used parts of chapters 2 and 6 in my presentation of the Marshall Sklare Memorial Lecture, in which I focused on a research agenda for future studies of the Jewish community in the United States. Sam Heilman and Bethamie Horowitz responded to that lecture with thoughtful and interesting ideas and suggestions. Part of my response to another session at those meetings, organized by Riv-Ellen Prell and revisiting my 1986 book *Jewish Continuity and Change,* incorporated some of the ideas in these lectures. Papers by Steve Cohen, updating part of my analysis of the 1975 Boston study, and by Sam Heilman, extending my discussion of residential concentration of the Orthodox, helped me to think through some of these ideas again.

I have also used some of the materials on ethnic continuities in presentations at colloquia organized by the Department of Sociology and the Population Studies and Training Center at Brown University. More formally, materials on ethnic categories were incorporated in the Watson Institute workshop on categorizing citizens organized by David Kertzer and Dominique Arel at Brown University, at a sociology colloquium on ethnic distinctiveness and assimilation in Israel at Stockholm University in 2002, and at a Social Science Research Council conference on immigration, religion, and civic life organized by Richard Alba and Albert Raboteau in Seattle in 2002. My presentation at Paideia–The European Institute for Jewish Studies in Sweden, organized by its director, Barbara Spectre, provided important feedback from European students. Colleagues and students attending these events helped me to sharpen my arguments and clarify my thinking as they challenged me on theoretical and empirical grounds. Many thought the arguments and ideas were interesting and convincing. I have benefited enormously from these reactions, criticisms, and suggestions. The final draft of these materials was prepared during my sabbatical at Stockholm University in the academic year 2001-2002. I am grateful to my colleagues at Brown University and to its administration for providing me with a sustained period of time to complete this draft.

I owe many debts of gratitude in the preparation of this book. My sincere appreciation to Paul Burstein, a sociologist at the University of Washington who has had a long-term interest in American and Israeli Jewish communities, for inviting me to Seattle and being one of my ardent supporters. Florence Katz and Paul graciously hosted Fran, my wife, and me for the duration of our stay in Seattle and Mercer Island. I have been charmed by the warmth of their family and their home. I am pleased to call them friends. And I am indebted to their children, Nathan, Anna, and Deborah, for being good sports about our intrusion into their lives.

Along with the world of Jewish scholarship, I am indebted to the Stroum family for their generosity and vision. Sam Stroum passed away during the period in which I rewrote and reorganized the lectures I had presented in May 2000. He was ill and undergoing medical treatment during my first two lectures but was able to attend the third. I was honored by his presence and by the presence of his wife and family, who attended the entire lecture series and were enthusiastic supporters. Sam has left many legacies to the Jewish world and has enriched the Program of Jewish Studies at the University of Washington by his generous support. May his memory continue to be a blessing.

I want to thank Naomi Sokoloff, then chair of Jewish studies at the University of Washington, who formally organized all the events surrounding the Stroum lectures and invited me to prepare these talks. She took care of all the details that made the lecture series run so smoothly.

Fran Goldscheider accompanied me, listened to the rehearsals of these lectures, and joined me for the talks themselves. She read over the penultimate draft of this book and made important suggestions for revisions. She has, over the years, tried to make sure that I say what I mean and that what I say makes some sense. She has been my most consistent critic, my most supportive colleague, and my loyal companion. For that and many things that are less appropriate to note in a preface, I love her.

Charles Hirschman is a distinguished demographer and sociologist at the University of Washington. Over the last decade or so, he has shared with me his wisdom and his insights about ethnicity and demography. Charlie initially challenged me to abandon the idea of a series of lectures that focused on the future by suggesting that studies of the future must be polemical by their very nature. I tried to disappoint him by not being polemical. He faithfully attended all the lectures, bringing along his father. Only occasionally did he close his eyes and nap. He was most serious in his attention and has always been warm and supportive. I am not sure he was convinced of the value of the lectures by the time they were completed and after he saw them again on University of Washington television. I cherish his friendship and respect his scholarly integrity.

I was fortunate to have studied with the late Nathan Goldberg. He was my mentor and professor at Yeshiva University and introduced me to the sociology and demography of the Jews in the 1950s. He taught me and hundreds of others that the biographies of great people are one of the key ways to study values. He was my inspiration and role model. I am most pleased to be able to carry on his sociological and demographic traditions. May his memory be a blessing for all of us working in the field of sociology and demography of the Jews.

Sidney Goldstein was my teacher and subsequently my colleague at Brown. Together we undertook one of the first systematic demographic studies of an American Jewish community and repeated it twenty-five years later. At times we have disagreed over the interpretation of the evidence about American Jews and how far we should go beyond the data. I cherish his friendship and his integrity. He remains the scholarly model for me and for all those who study American Jewish demography.

Alan Zuckerman, chair of the Department of Political Science at Brown and my faithful colleague and friend there, read through and discussed with me some of these lectures and, as always, showed me how I was unclear and often wrong. His work with me on our book *The Transformation of the Jews* in the 1980s remains one of the highlights of my intellectual career. I continue to draw freely from the sections of that book that he drafted. His friendship remains one of the important parts of my Brown experience.

My colleague in Judaic studies and history at Brown, Maud Mandel, has been the historian social scientists always need to have around. In courses that we taught jointly, at regular lunches, and in specific comments on the drafts of chapters, her criticisms were always gentle but correct, to the point, and helpful. One could not ask for a better colleague in Jewish history.

Saul Olyan, director of the Program in Judaic Studies at Brown, reviewed parts of chapter 5 and spared me several embarrassing errors. Lynn Davidman responded to an earlier version of chapter 4 by raising questions about biography and its uses in sociological research. She is an expert on the value of ethnographic work in the social sciences. I tried to sharpen my use of this methodology as a result of her insights and reservations. No doubt there is much more for me to learn about ethnography; this is a first attempt for a demographer. In this regard I have learned much from my doctoral students in anthropological demography, particularly Lacey Andrews, Susi Krehbiel, and Mara

Leichtman. They have tried to teach me the fine points of anthropology, with some resistance on my part. I still am trying to figure out what they mean by culture.

I mentioned to one of my former students at Brown, Gina Rhodes, and her friend Steve Wolfert, that I was writing a book about the Jewish future. They reminded me of Henrik Ibsen's 1890 play *Hedda Gabler* and how, in Act II, Lövberg announces to his friend that he is working on a new book that "deals with the future." His friend reacts suspiciously: "With the future! But, good heavens, we know nothing of the future!" Lövberg responds: "No; but there is a thing or two to be said about it all the same." I am grateful to them for guiding me to this revealing passage, for I, too, am writing a thing or two about a future that I know little about. Through Gina and Steve I want to acknowledge the help I have received over the years from my many wonderful students at Brown. They reinforce the application of a Talmudic aphorism: I have learned much from my teachers, but I have learned most of all from my students.

Besides dedicating this book to my mother, I dedicate it to her other two children (my brother, Harvey, and sister, Ethel) and their spouses (Judy and Eugene), her ten grandchildren (Judah and Avigaiyil; Elana, Aaron, Hillel, and Jeremy; Avi, Aryeh, Yoni, and Bracha), her twenty-one great-grandchildren—so far—and my six grandchildren—so far—Ben, Franny, Timothy, Atalya, Rosy, and Natan. With our help, they will design their own futures.

My grandson Michael did not live to read this book. His six days on earth (October 18–24, 2002) brought great joy to his family. His premature departure broke our hearts. May we remember the joy.

STUDYING THE JEWISH FUTURE

We are the only channel of Jewish tradition, those who must save Judaism from oblivion, those who must hand over the entire past to the generations to come. We are either the last, the dying, Jews or else we are those who will give new life to our tradition. Rarely in our history has so much depended upon one generation. We will either forfeit or enrich the legacy of the ages.

—Abraham Joshua Heschel, *God in Search of Man*

1

STUDYING THE JEWISH FUTURE

When I began to read and think systematically about how people have studied the Jewish future, I discovered that conceptions of the future were intrinsic to many studies of contemporary Jewish communities. Ideas and ideologies of the future appeared to me to be inherent in many studies of Jewish history as well. General, underlying theories about futures, conceptions of futures, and orientations toward futures often teach us how the past and the present have been interpreted. The identification of these implicit theoretical systems is fundamental to the study and exploration of futures.

In the introduction to his provocatively titled *A History of the Future,* the historian Warren Wagar wrote: "It was never my intention to predict the future. I cannot predict the future. Neither can you. I have placed my bets on a variety of outcomes. The future unveiled is not *the* future but an array of possibilities. Some are offered as warnings, others as utopias. Still others are projections of observable trends."[1]

The elements of the future that Wagar noted—that studying the future does not mean making predictions, that there are many possible futures, and that whereas some of these are projections of past trends, many are simply utopias or warnings—serve as abstract guidelines for my own explorations of the Jewish future. I do not predict the future of Jews and their communities but try to think through the range of issues that inform the future as it has unfolded over time and is likely to unfold in the decades ahead.

What does it mean to *study* the Jewish future? Studying the future means to examine the ways scholars have envisioned it, to ask how they have used their conceptions of the future to interpret past and contemporary Jewish communities, and to uncover the ideological assumptions underlying these conceptions. Studying the future requires outlining an array of possibilities and identifying some futures that are more likely than others. We cannot know with any certainty the direction in which the Jewish community is going. Even a casual acquaintance with modern Jewish history should warn us to modify our perspectives about accurate prediction. Yet Jews can steer a little better if they know where they would like to go and what hazards may be waiting during the passage. As a historian, Wagar emphasizes the futility of trying to reconstruct an "accurate" or "true" history. He reminds us that we cannot even fully "predict" the nineteenth century retroactively. All our histories are nothing more than models of a reality more complex than any human mind can encompass. Historical reconstruction is not the past itself but paintings of selected scenes of the past. So it is with the future.

Because none of us can know the full details of the past or even the present, we cannot, a fortiori, know the future. We are always in the process of rewriting history and reinterpreting the present. The unknowns of the future will be filled in by the next generation. Nevertheless, our explorations and reinterpretations of the past and the present lay the groundwork for thinking about the future. These cautions about our ability to understand the past and the present are important guidelines— indeed, humble reminders—as we think through the possible futures of Jewish communities. We are in a better position to know which futures are unlikely than to predict actual future patterns.

One theme that relates to studies of the future is the orientation one has to studying the past and the present. A central theme in my own orientation is to stress the value of comparative analysis. Most social scientists share the view that comparisons—over time, among groups, and between nations—are central to moving social science toward analysis and away from description. Our goals have been analytic and interpretive, although we often build up our analyses through rich descriptions. In studying the past, present, and future of Jewish communities, I have followed the comparative ideal. This orientation requires comparisons among Jewish communities, between Jewish and non-Jewish communities, and within communities over time. The ideal set of comparisons involves all three—comparing Jewish and non-Jewish communities over time and in relationship to one another. Not everyone has shared this research goal. Even among those who have argued for comparisons, few have been able to meet the challenges of a comparative agenda.[2] Nevertheless, I hope to demonstrate the value of such comparisons in studying the Jewish future. At the beginning of the twenty-first century, Jewish communities were concentrated in the United States, Israel, and several European countries. I focus on comparing these communities, past and present, as a basis for understanding the future.

A further introductory point relates to the importance of values in my assessment of the Jewish future. My major arguments about studying the future of the Jewish communities in the United States, Israel, and Europe focus primarily on the structural conditions of people's lives. These conditions shape, first and foremost, what people do—their behavior, the families they form, the networks that define their communities, the institutions they build and sustain. Yet I also incorporate an examination of the values Jews share as part of the cement that binds them to one another and to Jewish culture. I explicitly examine some of the sources of these cultural forms in religious texts and in the context of biography. I argue that the quality of Jewish life has become the key to the future of Jewish communities. Therefore, I explore Jewish values and hence the quality of Jewish life in the contexts of Jewish communities. The multiple meanings of Jewish culture emerge in the analysis that follows. But whatever we mean by the quality of Jewish life and by the culture or values that characterize Jewish communities, those values are always anchored in the structure of social life—in its institutions and social networks. Whatever is selected, constructed, and transmitted from the total array of Jewish cultural traditions will emerge from the contexts of Jewish life in families and community institutions.

I have a set of biases about how the past and present should be understood, and therefore about what is the likely future of Jewish communities. These are largely the biases of one form of social science; they do not reflect a Jewish ideological position. Certainly I care deeply about the Jewish community. I am committed to its future in constructive ways.

But I am less attached to a particular form of Zionist ideology or a uniform religious imperative or a secular humanist tradition. I have no particular ideological ax to grind, and I have not argued that others should follow a particular theme or philosophical agenda. Indeed, I have few prescriptive policies for others, since I think each of us should find his or her own way. And the diversity of paths taken by Jewish communities should be encouraged, not lamented or neutralized through attempts to culturally construct one worldwide Jewish community or nation. I have neither a utopian vision of the Jewish future nor a particular set of policy recommendations to ensure continuity or diversity. The details of my social science biases will become obvious as my argument unfolds, but it is primarily the bias of a researcher who can take "yes" as well as "no" for an answer to the question of whether there is a future for Jewish communities in open, pluralistic societies. It is a view based on the increasing interrelationships among Jewish communities generated not only by relocations and migrations but also by diverse and symmetrical exchanges in all directions. It is a bias founded on the interconnectedness of independent communities within an interrelated, more global community. My bias within the social sciences is that of a demographer, a sociologist, and a researcher who is committed to the centrality of theory and the critical value of empirical methodologies.

Most existing analyses of contemporary Jewish communities, their histories, and their futures are guided by one of three orientations. First, there is the Zionist framework, which views Jewish communities outside the State of Israel as eroding or declining. It emphasizes the role of anti-Semitism and discrimination in worsening the quality of Jewish life and the powerful impact of assimilation in reducing Jewish commitments. The Zionist bias focuses on Jewish nationalism as a source of Jewish continuity and as a solution to the Jewish condition in the "Diaspora." History and contemporary Jewish life are interpreted within this framework, and the Jewish future is clearly tied to the conditions of a Jewish-dominated, secular nation-state.

A second orientation emphasizes the religious basis of Jewish continuity. Judaism was the source of cohesion and values in the past and, it has been argued, should be the basis of a Jewish future. Secularization is among the many causes of a deterioration of Jewish communities.

The renewal of Jewish life therefore depends on rediscovering traditional religious values. Returning to Judaism—rediscovering or redesigning religious values—becomes, in this perspective, the challenge for a Jewish future. Spirituality and ritual observances become the protection against secularization and assimilation.

A third set of biases postulates that there is no future for Jewish ethnic values and community in the absence of discrimination. In this framework, religion is the past, and Zionism is ethnic nationalism, which will have no long-term impact on the future. Assimilation and universalism combine with individualism to cast the future without ethnic or religious distinctiveness. Rejecting both Judaism and nationalism, this orientation views (and celebrates) the Jewish future in the context of assimilation and cultural homogenization.

Selected parts of each of these three orientations inform my own orientation in studying the Jewish future. However, I reject all of these perspectives as sole guidelines for analysis. Instead, my presentation combines demographic and sociological analyses in historical and comparative perspectives. I have gone beyond the methodologies of both disciplines to search traditional Judaic texts and, in one case, an individual's biography for insights into Jewish values. These excursions border on the heretical, because I have crossed over into the humanities and beyond my competence as a social scientist researcher. I have done so cautiously and with intellectual uncertainty and discomfort. I am concerned that some of my social science readers will not appreciate this excursion into texts and biography, being fixated on empirical verification, hypothesis formation, and representativeness. I am even more concerned that historians and humanists will be dismayed by my social science empirical biases. Nevertheless, I have found these combined emphases engaging and helpful in shaping my thinking about futures.

I am sensitive to the issues of reading history and texts through the prism of the present—what some have called "presentism" or "reading history sideways."[3] So I have used texts and a biography in somewhat different ways from those who are experts on texts or ethnography, in order to highlight how these pieces of evidence might help us to understand the present. I do not study the texts and the biography as a way to understand them in their own contexts. My unease about these excur-

sions relates to the fundamental argument, which I have made repeatedly, that contexts count in understanding contemporary communities.
How can I not place the texts and the biography in their contexts? The
short answer is that I treat them not as objects to be studied in their own
right but as bases for understanding core Jewish values. At a minimum,
these methodological and substantive insights should pave the way for
a broader understanding of the use of sacred texts and biographies in
the social sciences.

My basic argument is that demographic and structural analyses are,
paradoxically, essential to dispel the notion that quantitative issues lie
at the heart of the challenge of future Jewish continuity. Numbers are
clearly the building blocks of community. But interpretations of demographic issues are often confusing and biased by ideological preconceptions. I raise these questions first in chapter 2 in the context of broad
arguments about population size and the demographic erosion associated with Jewish intermarriage. I attempt to show that intermarriage need
not be a demographic threat to the Jewish future, not because it should
be encouraged but rather because we need to understand the process
associated with marriage and family formation in different ways. From
a demographic point of view, the negative assessment of Jewish intermarriage is, I argue, misdirected and premature.

Population projections are one form of a contextualized vision of the
future. Social scientists and historians have used them as a basis for estimating future population sizes and structures. The goal is rarely to estimate population size for its own sake, but to suggest possible futures.
The assumption is that the size of a population has importance for families and communities, for different groups' power and influence.
Hence, the projection of the size of a population into the future becomes
a basis for thinking about a changed community. Often the assumption
is made that Jewish communal consensus is more likely to be generated by the "hard facts of demography" than by the more contentious
areas of religion, ethnicity, and Jewish culture. I argue in chapter 3 that
population projections are severely limited as a basis for studying the
core themes of the Jewish future. More importantly, I stress that the "hard
facts" are less "hard" and less "factual" than interpreters have made them
out to be. Population projections are limited by the vision of those who

prepare them. Some projections are limited by the way people use projections to bolster their ideological arguments about the future and the
present. Numbers are often intimidating to the uninitiated. I try to provide an assessment of the bases for Jewish population projections so that
we will better know how they are used and can better assess their strengths
and limitations.

Individual biographies inform us not about the future but about how
context shapes our sense of the future. In chapter 4, I present a biog-
raphical sketch to suggest how one person's conceptions of the future
were shaped by his life course and experiences. This man's story should
not be viewed as typical of Jewish biographies in the twentieth century;
none of them is representative. Rather, individual biographies reveal in
their details and in rich description how perspectives change as the community itself is transformed. I also think this particular biography is
interesting and captures some of the central themes of Jewish history
in the twentieth century. Many lessons can be drawn from this excursion. One abstract lesson is that our views of the future are powerfully
influenced by the communal contexts of our changing lives. It is important to reiterate that how we think about and study the future is not fixed
and inevitable. Our conceptions of the Jewish future are influenced by
our framework of analysis and our experiences and are likely to change
as the future unfolds. The future is not scripted and predetermined.

Texts—however esoteric—that have been defined as sacred in Judaism
can help us build constructively in defining and applying Jewish values.
In chapter 5, I attempt to illustrate this process by briefly examining animal sacrifices in the Hebrew Bible and reviewing how the prophetic tradition can be used to provide new insights into the quality of Jewish life
in the twenty-first century. I stress that I am less interested in the text
per se than in how it can be used to reflect on contemporary Jewish values. Grounding such values in Jewish texts legitimates their use for understanding the future of Jewish communities. My emphasis on sacred texts
does not necessarily mean that I am arguing for the belief in their sacred-
ness. Rather, historical and contemporary Jewish communities have
treated, and still treat, the texts as "holy." By using biblical texts I do not
want to imply that Judaism or its observance should be the primary basis
for strengthening the Jewish future. That may be the case for some Jews.

But most Jews everywhere are secular, and for them religion is unlikely to be the sole or primary source of Jewish culture. Rather, I use the texts to show the value of Judaism in its ethnic and Jewish cultural context. The Hebrew Bible reveals what we read into it. That seems to me always to have been the case. My examination of its texts, therefore, is not intended to interpret them in context but to read back into them the values that Jews think are important. I read the texts sociologically. Others have read and studied the textual tradition differently. I think that is what midrash, or exegetical commentary on the Hebrew Bible, is about. Perhaps my reading can be considered a sociological midrash.

In the final chapter, I return to the themes of the Jewish future by emphasizing the emergent ethnic and cultural foundations of contemporary Jewish communities in the United States, Europe, and Israel. My objective is to move from population numbers to other patterns of distinctiveness and to argue for the salience of Jewishness in addition to, or in lieu of, Judaism. In short, I want to show the power of Jewish culture, broadly defined. My goal is not to exclude Judaism from or replace it in studies of the future, but also not to limit the future to one of religion alone. The argument and analysis are my vision not of what *should* be but of what I understand as the contemporary pattern and its likely future trajectory.

Having reviewed and evaluated predictions of the futures of Jewish communities in the United States, Israel, and Europe, I suggest that these predictions or assessments are part of a set of theories about the end of the Jewish people in communities outside the State of Israel—the so-called Diaspora Jewish communities. I reject the lachrymose conception of Jewish history and its application to the social scientific study of contemporary Jewish communities.[4] In contrast, I present a more cheerful view of Jewish history and of the future of these communities. I am convinced that the evidence available on contemporary Jewish communities is more consistent with the latter view than with the former.

On the basis of an array of evidence, I conclude that the futures of these Jewish communities are much more secure than has been forecast in scholarly and popular publications. Not all Jewish communities, to be sure, have a positive future, but many do, and the largest are likely to have creative and distinguished futures. The key issue, I argue, is not the quantitative survival of the Jewish people, which I assess as being secure, but the quality of Jewish life. This assessment leads me to redefine Jewish quality. I reexamine the transformation of the Jews from a community defined along religious lines to a community that is primarily ethnic, defining ethnic in broadly structural and cultural terms. I argue that it is critical to study the broader cultural anchors of the Jewish community that have become critical in defining its future. I also suggest that an examination of culture forces us to examine the structural underpinnings of community. In particular, I emphasize the contexts of interaction and communal cohesion as the bases for Jewish continuity and cultural transmission. An examination of the forms in which the networks and institutions of the Jewish community operate suggests powerful bases of communal cohesion in transformed Jewish communities.

Throughout my research on the Jewish future I have been impressed by the increasing quality of the studies being carried out on Jewish communities. Such high standards have not always been the case. When Louis Finkelstein published his monumental collection on the Jews, and when Marshall Sklare prepared the first collection of materials on the sociology of the Jews, the study of contemporary Jewish communities was the stepchild of Jewish scholarship.[5] The last several decades have witnessed the publication of an enormous and rich set of studies of Jewish communities. I draw freely from these research efforts in my assessment of the Jewish future.

I have also been continuously disturbed by the uncritical uses of this research in its applied form. Policy planning is one way in which futures are manifested in the present, and the policy themes emergent in the Jewish community have been distorted by misunderstanding and ideological biases. My hope is that an alternative understanding of these patterns will generate new policies that will influence the future. Therefore, another goal of studying the future is to redirect its course so that some futures become more likely than others.

A reconsideration of a wide range of findings should not only inspire caution and modesty among policy planners but also, I hope, reorient policy makers to evaluate their biases. But that will not be enough if, in the process, the policies are not changed. No less importantly, identification of the hidden biases of previous research may make those who study Jews more open to exploring new avenues of research and new ways to study Jewish communities, their history, and their futures. I view change as representing challenge and transformation: it has the potential for creating new communities that are anchored in traditions but are not constrained by them. The best I can hope for is that social scientists, policy planners, and the Jewish community as a whole will recognize a new basis for optimism about the future of Jewish communities around the world. I am not naïve enough to believe that sound social scientific analysis will be used to re-create communities and redirect policies. I do not assume that policies will be responsive to research or even that they will be implemented in a voluntary community. Nevertheless, I am bold enough to assert that the current way of thinking is much too limited and distorting of the future possibilities of Jewish communities. The consideration of alternative futures would be sufficient reward for my efforts.

2

THE FUTURES OF JEWISH
COMMUNITIES IN THE UNITED STATES,
EUROPE, AND ISRAEL

What are the futures of contemporary Jewish communities in the United States, Europe, and Israel? No one knows. But in our understanding of the present and of trends in social life in the past, we have a strong foundation from which to conjecture about the possibilities. Our vision of the future is shaped by our understanding of the present in the context of the past, and our conception of the past is often shaped by our vision of the future. In addition, one of the many reasons we are curious about the future is that it informs us about what we can do now to prepare for, shape, and perhaps change what we expect will happen. Constructing images of the future allows us to think about how some aspects of the future that we envision can be prevented or altered so that they do not come about.

I begin my study of the Jewish future by reviewing the contemporary conditions of Jewish communities in the United States, Europe, and Israel. I survey the social fabric of contemporary Jewish communities in the context of their histories and as a basis for thinking about the next several decades. My review is designed as a corrective to some romanticized and ideologically driven conceptions of history and their projection into the future. I start with the United States, which had the largest concentration of Jews in the world at the beginning of the twenty-first century.

AMERICAN JEWISH COMMUNITIES

Jews in the United States are surviving; indeed, some entire Jewish communities are thriving. Contemporary American Jewish communities have resources, money, education, health, talent, organizations, and institutions on a scale unprecedented in historical memory. The survival of American Jews is less threatened by external forces than ever before. Most Jews in the United States have found unparalleled freedom and choice. And the amazing fact at the beginning of the twenty-first century is that when confronted with freedom and choice, most Jews choose to be Jewish rather than something else.

Half a century ago, who would have thought that Jews would be the most organized and institution-oriented ethnic-religious group in the United States, much less the wealthiest, best educated such group ever in that country, probably in the world, and probably ever in Jewish history? Just a generation ago, who would have believed that tens of thousands of Jewish students would be enrolled voluntarily in regular courses in Jewish subjects in hundreds of American colleges and universities? Who would have predicted that by the end of the twentieth century almost all American Jewish children would be exposed to some form of Jewish education? Who would have speculated that tens of thousands of Jewish students would be studying in a wide range of Hebrew day schools, or that more American students would be studying in yeshivas (religious academies) with American-educated rabbis and teachers than anywhere else at any time in history? In the early 1960s, few would have predicted that American Jews would share an almost universal consensus about the importance of the State of Israel in their lives, or that American Jewish continuity itself would be an organizing value shaping the communal agenda. Shared lifestyles, common background, similar educational levels, common culture, agreed-upon American goals about Israel and communal continuity, and extensive and diverse institutions and organizations cement the religious and ethnic distinctiveness of American Jews. As we move into the twenty-first century, the American Jewish community is characterized by an extraordinary array of qualities that portends well for its future.

One hundred years ago, at the beginning of the twentieth century, threats of pogroms and disenfranchisement, of blocked economic opportunity and discrimination, of anti-Semitism and race hatred, of migration, uprootedness, and foreignness, of poverty and financial uncertainty, of political revolution and displacement were central features of most Jewish communities in the world. Scattered, unorganized, stateless, and powerless, pressured by poverty, excluded by Christian (and Moslem) culture and church politics, ruptured by the upheavals of industrialization and urbanization, Jews a century ago thought they would be the last surviving generation. They were not. We are witnesses to the continuity of Jews as a community and as a people. The notion that contemporary Jewish communities are in the process of decline and disintegration is a powerful myth but, in the case of the United States, a poor and distorted description of the reality of Jewish life.

Jews have often been viewed as the ever-dying people—each generation in Jewish history sees itself as the last, from the ancient prophets to some contemporary historians, Zionists, and American Jewish Federation executives. This is a powerful story that has been institutionalized in some Judaic religious and secular holidays. It may motivate some people and institutions to support communal activities to save the dying remnants—or to despair about the future of the American Jewish community. But visions of decline are not sound descriptions of reality and are a distorting basis for thinking about the future. Furthermore, I believe the erosion theory of American Jewish life is destructive of Jewish culture and community. It is certainly a poor basis for communal policy and is inconsistent with the themes of renewal and constructive appraisal associated with some of the fundamentals of Judaism and Jewish culture. It is, I submit, poor social science and ideologically driven history.

The ashes of six million Jews destroyed in Europe and the sparks that reignited Jewish political control of Israel provided memory and anchors of identity to Jews everywhere at the end of the twentieth century. But beyond these historical convulsions, my question about the future of American Jewish communities relates to issues of social and cultural strengths within those communities. Are there internal communal dynamics that are sources of strength and that make survival as an American Jewish community worthwhile and desirable? This is not a question of whether American Jews will survive demographically, since there is every indication that they will in the future we can envision. The questions I think we should be asking are, What will be the quality of their Jewish life, and what will they transmit to the next generation? In part, for American Jews the questions become, Where and how will the next generation of Jews fit in with the emerging multicultural ethnic communities in the United States? Will they be indistinguishable from the white majority? Will their communities be less cohesive? Or will they form a strong community of ethnic and religious distinctiveness, marked off from others in the process of their integration and commitments to the United States? Which Jewish values will set the next generation apart from others in America?

Refocusing on the quality of American Jewish life may sound a little strange and exaggerated. Haven't we been informed repeatedly about the rapid demographic decline of American Jewish communities? Haven't we read reports about the assimilation of American Jews and the cultural erosion of their communities? Haven't we been presented with highlights of many studies that emphasize the unprecedentedly high intermarriage rates that seem to threaten the Jewish community's survival? Haven't we experienced Jewish intermarriages among our families, our children, and our friends? In the reporting of Jewish communal leaders, the numbers seem to convey that the younger generations are not getting married, or are marrying too late to have children of their own, or are marrying those who were not born Jewish. And those who do marry seem to be divorcing in record numbers. Indeed, who hasn't heard of deteriorating Jewish family values?

As part of the theme of erosion of the American Jewish community, many have focused on American Jews' apparent ignorance of Jewish culture. Haven't Jews often been embarrassed by their own Jewish ignorance, usually when non-Jewish friends, colleagues, or neighbors ask them to explain something about a Jewish holiday, a ritual, or a point of Jewish history or culture? Don't Jews hear regularly about their declining religious ritual observances and poor synagogue and temple attendance, as reported by social scientists and emphasized by religious leaders? Indeed, haven't Jews often questioned themselves about the *why* of Jewish survival? Perhaps too few Jews will be left in the next generation to reflect on the quality of American Jewish life. Will there be any basis for discussing Jewish quality of life among the surviving remnants?

Reading Jewish newspapers and periodicals reveals the "problems" that studies of American Jews have identified—what has been called the "severe crisis" of the "sinking" American Jewish community. One of my favorite articles appeared on the front page of the Sunday *New York Times* several years ago, focusing on the high rate of Jewish intermarriage and pointing to the conflict over the incorporation of the intermarried in the Jewish community. In a paragraph headed "Jewish population steadily declining," the article noted that "the American Jewish population has been steadily eroding from within." In fine print the text reported that Jewish population growth was 2 percent over the period of time measured. How population growth turns into steady decline and erosion is one of those Jewish miracles that cannot be explained. Ask rabbis and Jewish educators, Jewish communal leaders and organizational executives—the quality of Jewish life seems so clearly to be declining. Our communities are eroding, they say, and they seem to have the numbers to back them up.

Commentators and newspapers pick up on reports of crises and problems. But visions of decline are not confined to the popular Jewish press or to rabbis and communal leaders. Scholars of history and social science reiterate the theme. Here is what a professor of history at a major university wrote a few years ago in a book subtitled *The History of the Jews:* "In the case of the Jews the population trends signal the approaching end of Jewish history." He went on to argue that 85 percent of the Jews in the United States who were not Orthodox were "on a one-way ticket to disappearance as an ethnic solidarity." He continued: "Distinctive Jewish identity is running out as the largest, most affluent and vibrant Jewish community in the United States is demographically disappearing, not only through assimilation, the pathological breakdown of family life and failure to reproduce at the replacement level but through the racial suicide of a runaway rate of intermarriage. . . . The Jewish people as a whole, as an ethnic entity, are threatened with erosion and communal extinction. What the Holocaust began physically will in the twenty-first century be accomplished culturally."[1]

Another review at the end of the 1990s concluded that the American

Jewish population was "now headed for catastrophic decline." The math seems so simple: the author predicts that half of American Jews will disappear in two generations, because of high intermarriage and low fertility levels. He reports: "You start with 100 American Jews, you end up with 60. In one generation more than a third have disappeared, and in just two generations, two out of every three will vanish."[2] Three generations ahead—about a century—the future of the American Jewish community looks bleak indeed. With this forecast of demographic decline, it is no wonder the community is described as facing a crisis of internal deterioration. If the American Jewish community hasn't quite disappeared yet, so the argument goes, then the numbers seem to point to inevitable and serious demographic decline in a generation or two, and onward to a place in the dustbin of history.

In a 1964 article entitled "The Vanishing American Jew," *Look* magazine predicted the disappearance of the Jewish community in North America by the end of the twentieth century. And where is *Look* today? Yet even the most conservative estimate of Jewish population growth in the United States shows that Jewish population increased by 6 percent between 1976 and 1996.[3] What then is the basis of the demographic argument? Do we have enough confidence in the quantitative picture of the contemporary American Jewish scene to assess the demographic future? What do the numbers reveal? Are the prophets of doom and gloom correct in their assessment and interpretation of the evidence?

There is also the question of how Jewish culture will be affected by demographic decline and erosion. Clearly, the attitudes about crises and numbers can only reinforce the negative. Why should the next generation voluntarily stay on a sinking ship? If the children of Jews intermarry with non-Jews, what would attract their children to the Jewish community? If we keep on the same track, won't people choose to abandon even the weak forms of contemporary Jewishness, the declining Judaism and religious expressions, and the eroding Jewish community? Is there not a trajectory of inevitable numerical decline that cannot be stopped or reversed? These assessments of the future often appear to deliver a sharp and unambiguous message: Return to the good old days when intermarriage was rare, when families were large, when the home reinforced the values of Jewishness, when a "Jewish" language and culture filled the shops and people's lives, when synagogue attendance and religious observances were characteristic of the many rather than the few, when Jews' "values" were Jewish values and their families were probably wholesome and unquestionably Jewish. No matter the cost, so the message goes, these are the ideals Jews must live up to if they are to prevent the further deterioration of the Jewish community.

We do not have to be steeped in history to know that the good old days were in fact not so good. Nor do we have to be professional demographers and sociologists to understand that Jewish communities are not about to collapse and disintegrate in this or the next generation. The contemporary American Jewish community cannot be described as disappearing or eroding, and it seems to display significant indications of vibrancy and vitality. How might we best reconcile these different views of the future of the American Jewish community?

My interpretation of the evidence on the quantitative survival of American Jewish communities as the twenty-first century begins is that some communities are thriving as never before, even as others are diminishing. Some communities are using their resources to enhance the quality of their Jewish lives and the Jewishness of the next generation, and others are not. Some segments of the Jewish community are more Jewish than ever before, whereas others have melted into the pot called America. Some Jews are undoubtedly lost to the community through assimilation, whereas others are entering it through marriage and renewed Jewish identification. As a result of these contradictory and clashing tendencies, new sources of strength may be emerging from what is often viewed as weakness, as in the case of intermarriages that lead to new Jewish commitments among those not born Jewish. Even in the stronger, more cohesive Jewish communities, some individuals are moving out while others are moving in. So if you look for the negative you will find it, and you will have some numbers to back you up. But you will miss the positive, which shows that the negative numbers do not tell the complete story. If you look at the whole, you will see a balance, a transformed American Jewish community that is both encouraging and challenging for the future. In this sense, both the views about decline and those about renewal are correct. They are simply referring to different parts of the community and to different indicators of group cohesion.

My view is based on an assessment of the changes that have occurred over the generations and an interpretation of the rich but complex information we now have available. It is a more optimistic than pessimistic view of the Jewish future. I reject the phrasing of the question, as some have put it, whether the glass is half full or half empty. It is a distortion when we see only half a glass, when we examine only part of the evidence and emphasize only the negative aspects of a culture. Most importantly, we need to examine what is in the glass, that is, what the quality of Jewish life is. It is the contents of the glass even more than the volume it holds that we need to explore and rethink. And social scientists and Jews themselves have rarely used the information available to measure, analyze, and evaluate the quality of Jewish life. It seems that Jewish leaders see half a glass of Jewish life without identifying its changing content. They often focus on selected parts of Jewish communities and on just segments of the lives of Jews living in them. Some historians and social scientists measure Jews' current lives against a nostalgic construction of their past, which often distorts the past and misdirects appraisals of the future.

I want to explore the interpretations of the numbers and develop some basis for beginning to comprehend the enormous transformations that have brought American Jews where they are today. At the same time I want to generate a new way of thinking in order to influence policy, to tip the balance toward a richer Jewish quality of life within a voluntary but tightly bound community in the future. I start with one theme that has become an obsession with American Jewish communal leaders, some social scientists, and many journalists and Jewish parents: intermarriage.

Intermarriage

For a community to survive and to flourish, it needs, at the most elementary level, generational renewal. And an ethnic or religious group requires particular attention to generational replacement, because institutions alone are insufficient to ensure survival. Without people, institutions become heirlooms to be examined in museums, relics of the past, interesting artifacts for archaeologists and historians. Judaism and Jewish culture and religion should be living fountains, not relics of the past. For continued survival, those who represent the institutions of the Jewish community must be concerned about demographic continuity. And in the American context, generational renewal is anchored in the family.

The American Jewish family has changed so much in the last several decades that people's great-grandparents would scarcely recognize it. Reductions in the sizes of families, delays in the timing of marriage, increases in nonmarriage, cohabitation, and divorce, significant proportions of time spent living independently, often alone, away from family, and the new balance between work and family emerging among women and men are among the most conspicuous family changes among Jews and others in the United States. In the context of the changed family and pressures for ethnic continuity, American Jews confront what some consider the greatest threat yet to emerge in the contemporary period: intermarriage between Jews and non-Jews. It appears that such intermarriage directly reflects the extent of assimilation of the community, threatens demographic renewal, and inevitably leads to a weakening of Jewish cultural continuity. All of these negative implications of intermarriage appear obvious and can be easily accepted when just the rates of intermarriage are presented. The implications are understood intuitively from the rates and their increases over time. In general, however, I think that the Jewish community's concern with intermarriage is misdirected, and that the threat is more apparent than real. Let me explain.

During most of the twentieth century, Jewish intermarriage rates were low, but the phenomenon was devastating to the Jewishness of those who intermarried and to the Jewish community. People who intermarried repudiated their religion, their families, and their communities. And their religion, families, and communities abandoned them. Although the numbers were small, those lost to the Jewish community were not only the intermarried themselves but also their children and subsequent generations. Most Jewish parents at the end of the twentieth century had grown up in communities where intermarriage was rare, where the intermarried were largely Jewish men married to non-Jewish-born women, where conversions to Judaism were not encouraged and often were seriously discouraged, and where intermarried couples and their children were not accepted members of the Jewish community. So the historical basis for the obsession of the American Jewish community with intermarriage as a threat is understandable.

However, the context of American Jewish communities and the circumstances of the family lives of American Jews have changed in the last several decades, and so have the rates of intermarriage. To understand the changing family and its impact on intermarriage, we need to appreciate the Americanness of Jews in the United States and their integration into modern American society. The changing integration of American Jews has been associated with increasing social contacts between Jews and others. Our modern world has opened choices in residence, jobs, and marriage. The move toward non-Jewish circles is particularly conspicuous in choices of spouses and neighbors. Intermarriage has become less exceptional, less an issue of alternative religious discovery or of political or economic necessity (as it often was in the past and in European countries). Intermarriage between Jews and non-Jews has become a reflection of routine interaction among individuals. These relationships are an integral part of the daily lives of American Jews. In this sense, intermarriage has become embedded in American Jewish culture and family life. Marrying someone of a different ethnic or religious background has become consistent with the way Jewish parents and their children live.

Social scientists focus on intermarriage between Jews and non-Jews precisely because it symbolizes the extent of Jewish-non-Jewish interaction, the weakening of Jewish culture, and, by inference, the potential weakening of the Jewishness of the community. It directly addresses the question of the centrality of Jewish values and the content of those values. The fundamental demographic issue in a voluntary community is who is a member of the community. Being Jewish in the United States and being part of the community is a question not only of who one marries but also of who is in the Jewish group, of the Jewishness of one's descendants, and hence of the demographic continuity of the community. In the United States, by and large, Jewish group membership is voluntary, based on a social definition, not a biological or a religious legal one. It is informal, not formal, group membership, but it is no less powerful for its informality. Among the concerns within the community is, Where do those who are socially, informally, or newly Jewish fit?[4]

The evidence shows that most American Jews continue to be Jewish by the standard of having been born to Jewish parents. But increasingly there are new Jews in the United States, that is, persons who become Jewish through commitments to their newly formed families and their identification with the Jewish community. The process of becoming Jewish by having a Jewish home and identifying with the Jewish community, as well as the formal process of conversion to Judaism, varies over the life course. Jewish identification often increases as families are formed and children need to be educated. And the major source of Jewish identification for American Jews tends to be ethnic or communal and not narrowly religious. So in a real sense, the issue affecting Jewish continuity in the context of higher intermarriage rates is not intermarriage per se but the Jewishness that characterizes families and households. Formulating this issue as a question, we need to ask, How do people who are raised in Jewish families and those who choose to identify as Jews conduct their lives, raise their children, and connect to their extended families and the broader community that is Jewish? Moreover, what is the Jewish content (the quality of Jewish life) in households in which some but not all members define themselves as Jewish? That is, what is the Jewishness of households shared by Jews and non-Jews?

What are the facts, as we know them? There is no question that rates of intermarriage between Jews and non-Jews have increased over time in the United States. Although the exact level is unknown, it probably varies nationally between 40 and 50 percent of those who married in the period 1990–2000. (The intermarriage results of the National Jewish Population Survey of 2000–2001 have not yet been released as of 2003, but the rate is likely to remain as high as that of the 1990 survey.) There is a considerable range among communities in the level of intermarriage, but again the detailed evidence is weak, because migration between communities is high. It is also unclear whether the small size of a particular Jewish community fosters intermarriage or whether the intermarried are more likely to move to areas of lower Jewish population density. Thus, while regional and state-level variations in intermarriage rates are expected, researchers have been unable to disentangle the effects of community size and composition from the selection of community type among the intermarried.

In the past, Jewish men married out more than did Jewish women. There is some evidence suggesting that gender differences in inter-marriage have diminished considerably in the recent period. Since women tend to take a more active role in the home, the gender differ-ence was the basis for more concern in the past, because the non-Jewish-born spouse would, presumably, be more likely to define the Jewishness of the home. Similarly, it is likely, though unexplored empirically, that Jewish women who marry out may encourage the Jewishness of the home—perhaps more so than Jewish men who marry out. Hence, the changing gender pattern of intermarriage may have a more positive effect on the Jewishness of the home today.

There is also no simple association between intermarriage and alien-ation from the Jewish community. Over the last two decades, it is likely that generational continuity of Jewishness among the intermarried has actually increased. That is, more children raised in households in which one or more persons were not born Jewish have remained Jewish in a variety of ways as they formed their own families. This new pattern is connected to the increased levels of intermarriage and conversions and to the increased acceptance of the intermarried among families and within the Jewish community.

What happens to the children of those who marry out? Are they always lost to the Jewish community? Doesn't the high rate of Jewish inter-marriage imply a decrease in the Jewishness of children and an increase in the non-Jewishness of intermarried households? Don't the simple numbers reveal that high rates of intermarriage threaten Jewish demo-graphic continuity in the United States?

I try to answer these questions about the future by examining a model of intermarriage over two generations. Table 1 is an exercise or simulation. The information it contains is designed to answer, at least hypothetically, the question about the demographic effects of high inter-marriage rates in the intermarrying and second generations. Since we have no accurate numbers for these patterns, I have estimated the num-bers largely on the basis of available statistics, in order to illustrate some popular misconceptions in understanding intermarriage rates.

In this illustration, the community begins with fifteen Jews by birth in the first generation, or cohort, and gains two spouses by conversion.

TABLE I

Intermarriage and Generational Continuity
in Two Hypothetical Jewish Cohorts

Couple	First Generation	Second Generation
1	Jew + Jew	Two Jews
2	Jew + Jew	Two Jews
3	Jew + Jew	Two Jews
4	Jew + Jew	Two Jews
5	Jew + Jew	Two Jews
6	Jew + non-Jew, converted	Two Jews
7	Jew + non-Jew, converted	Two Jews
8	Jew + non-Jew, unconverted	One Jew and one non-Jew
9	Jew + non-Jew, unconverted	Two non-Jews
10	Jew + non-Jew, unconverted	Two non-Jews

NOTE: Number of first-generation Jews = 15; number of second-generation Jews = 15.

(In reality, 20–25 percent of non-Jewish-born spouses convert in religious ceremonies, and it is reasonable to suppose that another 15 percent identify themselves as Jewish without formal religious conversion.) So we begin with ten couples, of which half consist of spouses who are both Jewish by birth. Seventy percent of the couples, then, are Jewish either by birth or by religious conversion. The intermarriage rate is 33 percent for individuals (five out of fifteen) and 50 percent for couples (five out of ten), and the rate of conversion is 40 percent. Examining individuals rather than couples reveals that of the fifteen born Jews in this cohort, ten are postulated to be married to other born Jews. With fifteen born Jews and two conversions to Judaism, we have a demographic gain of two Jews in this generation.

One clear implication of this simulation for the first generation is that the Jewish community can achieve demographic gains with an individual rate of intermarriage of 33 percent and a couple intermarriage rate of 50 percent. At the postulated rate of religious conversion, when one-third of the Jews marry non-Jews and one half of the couples consist of Jews married to born non-Jews, the Jewish community *gains* two addi-

tional Jews. If we think of Jewish continuity as based not solely on religious conversion but also on ethnic identification, then the prospects
for gain, stability, and continuity in the context of high intermarriage
rates are reinforced. In short, high individual or couple intermarriage
rates do not necessarily result in demographic decline in the generation
that is intermarrying.

I have argued that the key issue for group continuity is generational
renewal. What happens to the second generation, the children of the intermarried, under a regime of high rates of intermarriage? We have no clear
empirical answers, but if we continue with this exercise, the results may
be as surprising for the second generation as they were for the first. For
the second generation, I assumed that each couple in the first generation had two children. The results show that the number of Jews in the
second generation is exactly the same as that in the first generation—
fifteen. How did this come about? I assumed that each of the Jewish-
born couples had two Jewish children and each of the Jewish families
in which one partner was converted had two Jewish children. I also
assumed that only one of the six children of Jews married to unconverted
Jews were Jewish. The result of these combined assumptions was generational stability in the size of the Jewish group, despite a high rate of
intermarriage.

Of course, much depends on the third and subsequent generations
and their rates of intermarriage, identification, and conversion. Evidence
for such third-generation children is simply unavailable (we barely have
systematic evidence for the second generation). There is little that is
inevitable about the Jewishness of this generation. Nor can we assume
that family size patterns and Jewish conversion or identification rates
will remain the same. The exercise is designed not to predict the impact
of intermarriage on the Jewish community but simply to demonstrate
that the implications of high rates of intermarriage are not predetermined
or obvious. The future of the Jewish community under high rates of intermarriage is therefore a direct consequence not of intermarriage itself
but of the extent to which the intermarried are incorporated into the community through either conversion or the Jewish identification of the non-
Jewish-born partners. Perhaps the key is the Jewishness of the home,
not the marriage pattern. Simply put, it is not whom one marries but

how the intermarried build their homes and raise their children that counts demographically.

The primary lessons to be learned from this simulation are twofold. First, high intermarriage rates for individuals and couples *may* result in population stability when conversions occur or when non-Jewish-born partners identify with the Jewish community. More importantly, even with high rates of intermarriage, the community maintains overall numerical stability when many children are raised as Jews. Intermarriage itself does not directly challenge Jewish continuity demographically. The future impact of Jewish intermarriages on the Jewish population in the United States will reflect the extent to which Jewishness is an integral and important part of Jewish homes and families.

Second, a generational perspective is needed to identify those who are raised as Jews and who grow up to be Jewish and start Jewish families. The policy and communal questions become, How do we encourage parents in mixed Jewish-non-Jewish families to raise their children Jewishly? Who will want to be Jewish when they form families of their own? How much does acceptance of the intermarried by the Jewish community facilitate the eventual Jewishness of these people's homes and children?

A final thought to be considered: What would be the outcome if half of the children of the three intermarried, unconverted families were raised as Jews, rather than only one of the six children of these couples? The Jewish community would gain two additional Jews over the original fifteen of the first generation, repeating the first generation's numerical gain. I should note that the actual figures, as of 1990, seem to be that about 40 percent of the children of Jewish intermarriages are clearly identified as Jewish in terms of their ethnic or religious identity or both, and 40 percent are identified by their parents as non-Jewish. Twenty percent are identified as uncommitted. What the children will become Jewishly as they grow up to have families of their own is open to speculation. And much depends not on what has occurred up to this point in American Jewish history but on what is done to shape the American Jewish future.

What can we conclude from these surprising implications? It is clear that formal conversion to Judaism is one important path to raising Jewish children. But it is not the only path. There are large numbers of non-Jewish-born persons who identify themselves as Jews and who are identified as Jews by their families, friends, and Jewish communities, without formal conversion. They are members of families and households that are defined as Jewish. Through marriage and the setting up of households, many born non-Jews are engaged in family, communal, and organizational activities that are Jewish. Moreover, there is increasing evidence that nonconversion at the time of marriage does not foreclose the possibility of religious conversion to Judaism at a later date. Jewish identification and practices at the time of marriage do not remain constant over the life course. Therefore, it is not necessarily marriage or a particular religious ceremony held at the time of marriage that fosters subsequent Jewish commitment. It is the context of the household and family, of doing things Jewishly, that creates the potential for raising the next generation Jewishly and, in turn, for demographic continuity.

It is important to reiterate that the Jewishness of the home should not be measured only according to religious practices or ritual observances. (I return to this theme in chapter 6.) This is the case, too, for the Jewishness of couples in which both spouses were born Jewish. (If religious observances were the only criteria, then few born Jews in the United States and Israel would be very Jewish.) Rather, family, communal, and associational *networks* are the key indicators of Jewish continuity. Institutions are community ways of organizing these networks. Nevertheless, even if religious affiliation were the only criterion, it is clear that many intermarried Jewish couples, if not the majority of them—including those who do not convert religiously—identify with a temple or synagogue, attend temple services, and perform religious rituals only slightly less than do born Jews married to born Jews.

Thus, intermarriage and disengagement from the Jewish community are no longer synonymous. Since those who intermarry are often only somewhat less attached to the Jewish community and only somewhat less Jewish in their behavior and commitments, increasing rates of intermarriage by themselves are poor indicators of the weakening quality of Jewish life. Intermarriage is not necessarily the final step toward total assimilation. In most intermarriages, the Jewish partner remains attached in some ways to the Jewish community, unlike in the past. Also, unlike in the past, the non-Jewish-born partner is likely to become attached to the Jewish community in at least some ways. In many cases, the children of the intermarried identify Jewishly through family, friends, neighborhood, and Jewish organizational ties. Many of their friends are Jewish, many support Israel, and many identify themselves as Jews. Most have important relationships with their Jewish relatives. And some proportion of spouses and their children formally convert to Judaism, becoming Jewish under the direction of rabbis and their institutions.

In conjunction with the increasing rate of intermarriage in the United States has come an increasing acceptance of the intermarried by Jewish families and by the secular and religious institutions of the community. Unlike in the past, the intermarried are more likely to be accepted and even welcomed in the Jewish community. Rarely is inter-marriage greeted nowadays with the Jewish mourning rituals of sitting shiva or reciting kaddish, as families often responded to it earlier in the twentieth century. Altogether, then, the research evidence shows that the intermarried cannot be written off as lost to the Jewish people. Their families have not written them off, many of their rabbis have not writ-ten them off, Jewish organizations have not written them off, and they have not written themselves off (although some social scientists, histo-rians, and policy makers seem to have dismissed their role in the future of the Jewish community).

Therefore, the increasing rate of intermarriage among American Jews does not necessarily mean erosion of the Jewish community, except through the prism of the segregated Orthodox and that of some Israeli Jews who reject the possibility of Jewish continuity outside of Israel. Intermarriage may even imply strength when significant proportions of the intermarried are actively involved in being Jewish and practicing Judaism. Intermarriage rates unambiguously mean that large networks of Jews are touched, affected, and linked to the intermarriage issue. That is, the proportion of Jews connected to the intermarried is larger than the proportion who actually make up intermarried couples. Hardly a Jewish household in the United States has not experienced intermar-riage through a family member, a neighbor, or a friend. Even those who have not been affected directly by intermarriage are therefore concerned about the future shape of the Jewish community in American society. The increase in intermarriage such that it now encompasses most of the Jewish community has been the critical family transformation among American Jews over the last several decades.

Whether intermarriage should be treated as a sign of erosion of the American Jewish community depends on the commitments of the inter-married to that community and the eventual commitments of their children. Much depends as well on how Jewish families and formal religious and secular institutions accept and nourish linkages between those born Jewish and those Jewish by identification, commitment, or conversion. One perspective to consider is what attracts the "other," the non-Jew, to the Jewish community and its values. It is less likely to be the religious attractions of Judaism than the social qualities of Jewishness. We shall encounter this theme again in a subsequent chapter.

It is also important to view the issue of intermarriage from the perspective of the next generation. Young Jewish adults are raised with positive values of family and community and struggle with the question of how the community and the family will enhance the acceptance of new Jewish and non-Jewish family members. While marriage may be based on individual decision making and considered the result of romantic love and individual choice, marriage continues to link families together. In turn, families are the basis of community. So marriage and the formation of new families are critical for the quality of Jewish life.

The evidence as a whole suggests that the American Jewish community is continuing to survive, and I suggest that some parts of it are thriving as the twenty-first century begins. To stress the quality of Jewish life, we must begin to reorient our perspective to emphasize that the Jewish community in the United States is not eroding and disintegrating. American Jewish culture is vibrant and creative and thoroughly American. And that culture has the potential to reach a wider range of people and attract the next generation, if it can meet certain challenges. The next generation can relate to the Jewish community better when the community is viewed as viable and constructive. When Jewish communities and families are supportive of the positive values of Jewish culture and history, there is a greater likelihood of continuity. When Jewish culture and Judaism in their diverse forms are attractive to the younger generation, the community has a greater probability of survival. When adult children are connected to family and to Jewish institutions, then they, too, can appreciate the value of forming a Jewish home of their own. Their family patterns are more likely to result in Jewish commitments when members of the Jewish community are defined more by their social connections and cultural activities than by their biological roots.

Families and Networks

One of the implications of this exercise in studying intermarriage generationally is that we need to focus on families and not primarily on individuals. It is ironic that the American Jewish family has been at the center of sociological (and theological) thinking for decades but is treated superficially in research. We sociologists have designed our research to focus mainly on individual identity in a family vacuum, obtaining survey information about one respondent rather than from all adult family members. When we have focused on the family, we have tended mainly to measure childbearing or marriage, and not family relationships. We have rarely studied children when they were not living at home, and we have not explored the processes leading to the formation of new Jewish family unions. We have studied marriage as a "status" (as in "marital status") but have rarely explored family structure (e.g., the timing of marriage) and process (e.g., the formation of extended family relationships). We have argued theoretically for the power of networks as a basis of ethnic continuity but have not collected information on family networks. We argue about generational changes (by which we mean distance from the immigrant generation) without focusing on intergenerational family relationships or life-course transitions (e.g., to adulthood, to the empty nest). These elementary family themes have not been systematically addressed in empirical studies of contemporary Jews, even though they are at the core of communal life among voluntary ethnic and religious groups in the United States.

Our implicit theory and expectation is that Jewish family life has "declined" over time, by which we mean that the configuration of the nuclear family has changed. Social science research has bemoaned the disintegration of the Jewish family for over a century. To rephrase Simon Rawidowicz, we have made the assumption of an "ever-declining Jewish family" and have selectively organized and interpreted our data to fit our preconceptions.[5] We should, instead, study families to investigate how they *strengthen* Jewish communities. At a time characterized by increasing divorce, remarriage, and cohabitation, we have assumed that new family forms have only negative implications for group cohesion. Therefore, we have failed to design studies of reconstituted families, step-families, and their children, grandparents, and other extended family members. We often know about extended family members among Jews only in the crude, stereotypical forms of popular culture. Rarely have we systematically studied patterns of interaction among extended family members.

We have incorporated "gender" by examining the differences between men and women. That is clearly inadequate.[6] Systematically incorporating the gender dimension requires that we examine *relationships* between men and women in the same way that we need to explore intergenerational relationships between parents and children. Gender and generational relationships need to be related to an examination of the religious and ethnic institutions and organizations in the community. They are also a basis for studying what is happening in Jewish homes. We have a considerable literature that has stereotyped Jewish mothers and fathers, grandparents and siblings, but we have developed little sound social scientific research investigating these roles.

Focusing on families reminds us that the family is the unit in which generational continuities are critical, but the Jewish family has been radically changing. On the continuity side, the family is where Jewish culture has placed its emphasis, in terms of religious and cultural activities and the division of labor within the household, between generations, and in the separate spheres of men and women. Family also means children and social and economic networks. The radical changes in the family over the last several decades are challenges to the culture of the Jewish community and its cohesion. But radical changes in the family do not necessarily imply erosion, decline, and disintegration, because new family relationships emerge which are different from those of the past but which may strengthen the future.

Furthermore, think about Jewish college students, who, in the first decade of the twenty-first century, are more likely than not to attend college away from home and live separately from their parents for long periods of time before they marry. Think about widowhood, and how women are more likely than men to spend a significant number of years living alone rather than in intergenerational households. Think of stepparenthood and blended families, which require new ways to reconfigure the power of family relationships intergenerationally. Clearly, the conception of the family of a century ago cannot be the basis of our study of the Jewish future.

The major family theme that has been written about is that of marriage patterns between Jews and others, in an attempt to reveal the "problems" of intermarriage. The obsession of the Jewish community and some social scientists with the intermarriage question should be the *object* of our study rather than the basis of our interpretation. We know embarrassingly little about intermarriages, particularly given the hundreds, perhaps thousands, of articles and reviews that have been written about them. We know even less about the family patterns that emerge subsequent to marriage. We have a few preliminary studies about the children of the intermarried, but no serious longitudinal data and no details about the choices made by the intermarried. Thus, we have not studied the consequences of intermarriage (although we tend to write endlessly about them), because we have not followed up on intermarried families to examine the critical question of the quality of their Jewish family life. The list of unresearched questions is almost endless.

We assume that intermarriages result in a decline in the quantity and quality of Jewish communities and then use the data on rates of intermarriage to support our preconceived notions. But as I have shown, there is an equally plausible set of interpretations that lead to an opposite conclusion. Even with high rates of intermarriage for individuals and couples, quantitative gains to the Jewish community are likely, depending on the extent to which non-Jewish-born persons identify with and are accepted by the community. And gains to the community may continue in the second generation, depending again on the ways in which families raise their children. Unfortunately, we have only simulation models to demonstrate these counterintuitive demographic points, because we have not traced identity changes over the life course or followed through on how the children of the intermarried identify themselves when they form families. Nor do we know how these patterns have evolved over the last several decades as the intermarried have become more accepted by Jewish institutions and networks of Jewish relatives and as their children have increasingly been the children of Jewish mothers rather than Jewish fathers. Hence, intermarriage does not have the same meaning in the new context of family relationships as it did in the older context of rejection and escape. We have not begun to consider how intermarriage relates to the question of the quality of Jewish life.

The issue is not which argument about intermarriage is correct. Without new thinking about the generational impact of Jewish intermarriages, we will continue to reiterate our biases rather than study the future of Jewish families. We certainly should be wary about projecting the consequences of intermarriage for the future demography of Jewish communities without considerably more research. I discuss the entire issue of Jewish population projections in the next chapter. No less important than the demographic rethinking that is needed in studying the Jewish future is the need to explore the qualitative significance of the changing meanings of Judaism and Jewish culture.

ARE EUROPEAN JEWISH COMMUNITIES VANISHING?

My assessment of the future of the American Jewish community is that it will arise from an existing community that is ethnically vibrant and demographically stable. Do similar patterns characterize Jews and their communities in contemporary Europe? How will the unique features of European Jewish communities after the Holocaust influence their likely futures? Is there any basis for postulating that European Jewish communities are demographically stable at the end of the twentieth century or that they are likely to thrive in the future?

European Jewish communities are significantly different today from the way they were after World War II. Do they have a sufficient basis on which to build and flourish in the next generation? To this question, there is only one answer: Some European Jewish communities have the potential for growth and development, whereas others have declined in size and are likely to lose further size and cohesion in the future. This conclusion parallels my findings for American Jewish communities, although the number of cohesive European communities is smaller, and changes over the last several generations have been more profound in Europe. There has also been a shift in the locations of European Jewish communities that have the potential for continuity and growth.

The demographic consensus is that European Jewish communities in the post-Holocaust period confront erosion and decline even more severe than that confronting communities in the United States. European Jewish communities have been seen largely through the prism of the Holocaust and Zionist ideology—that is, the Holocaust is viewed as a severe form of anti-Semitism, and Zionism adds in the projected assimilation and disappearance of Jews in countries of the Diaspora. They have also been measured relative to the large and vibrant Jewish communities of eastern Europe at the turn of the twentieth century. The decline in the number of Jews and the destruction of their religious and secular communal institutions, combined with major emigration and upheavals in eastern Europe, have resulted in a description of the Jews in Europe since 1945 as the "vanishing Diaspora."[7]

Major researchers of European Jewry echo what has been predicted about American Jews (and vice versa). A Jewish social scientist at Oxford University, reviewing the results of a conference on European Jewry and some demographic data, argues that the community of Jews in Europe is disintegrating and that emigration is the next step toward the end of European Jewry. He says, "There are still large segments of the Jewish people [of Europe] who, as in the past, are 'sitting on packed suitcases,' ready to leave the country where they are living. For the Jewish people, it seems that the age of large-scale migration is not yet over."[8]

In a book on the future of the Jews, David Vital, the Zionist historian, dismisses the future of European Jewry. Even where Jews have prospered in Europe, he states, their very success makes these communities of Jews "ever weaker and ever more diluted." They "do no more than persist." The reason for their "endemic weakness" is "material and quantitative." They are "too small to sustain full societies. Thus, the Jewries of Europe are subject to steady erosion, if not decay."[9]

A major Jewish historian asserts that European Jews as a group face a clouded future. He argues: "We witness now the end of an authentic Jewish culture in Europe. The prospects for collective survival are dim. . . . We now witness the withering away of Judaism as a spiritual presence. . . . Jewish culture in the sense of traditional religious learning has already been virtually eliminated from Europe. . . . Jews in Europe now face a similar destiny [to that of the Jews of Kai-Feng China]. Slowly but surely they are fading away. Soon nothing will be left save a disembodied memory."[10]

It is unclear what the definition of "authentic" Jewish culture or "traditional" Jewish learning would be. To be sure, the Europe of the nineteenth century and its Jewish communities are no longer. The religious institutions that dotted the landscape of eastern Europe have been destroyed or relocated. European Jewish communities and their institutions are no longer central in the configuration of world Jewry or in creative Jewish religious and secular political culture, as they were a hundred years ago. In large part, the European Jewish communities' foundation of poverty and oppression, of political anti-Semitism and discrimination, has also faded. The United States and Israel—both with strong Jewish European roots—have become the new centers of Jewish culture and religion. Nevertheless, we do not yet have a grasp on whether the changes, the "differences" over time, have moved European Jewish communities in the direction of "vanishing" or whether these communities have simply been transformed into something different from what preceded them but with a new potential for growth and development.

What do demographic trends reveal about European, including Russian, Jewish communities? Here, too, we have a weak statistical base and some difficult comparisons to make. In discussing trends in the European Jewish population, a strategic question is, What are the most salient points in time for which we should make comparisons? Most historians and demographers who view the Holocaust as central for understanding contemporary European Jewish communities start from 1939. Their comparisons show the enormous demographic toll of the Holocaust and the subsequent decline in European Jewish populations.

That is of course a valid perspective, and the numbers are indisputable. The Jewish population of Europe in 1939 was 9.6 million, and in 1946 it was estimated at 3.9 million. By the mid-1990s it had declined further, to little more than two million. This decline largely reflected post-war emigration from Europe to Israel and the United States. Some Zionists migrated, as did many surviving religious Jews, and those who were willing to remain in or return to countries where Jews had been killed tended to be relatively secular and assimilated. Furthermore, the remnants of European Jewry are an older and aging population with few sources of generational renewal. The numbers, then, are consistent in broad outline with what we know happened to European Jewish communities during and after the Second World War. But although the past is often a guide to the future, there may be signs of community renewal among European Jews. Past demographic patterns are not inevitable predictors of the future. Demography is not destiny.

And the whole demographic story has not been told. What if we moved our comparisons back in time? What if we started with 1800 and assessed longer-term Jewish population trends in Europe? What if we took into account not just the Holocaust but also immigration from eastern Europe to western Europe and the United States in the fifty years prior to the 1920s? What if we reexamined immigration from Russia and the rest of the former Soviet Union from the 1970s through the 1990s, seeing it not only as a loss of Russian Jews but as a gain to other Jewish communities? Then the interpretation of the demographic picture becomes more complicated. In 1800 there were two million Jews in all of Europe, about the same figure as in the mid-1990s. On the face of it, this is remarkable demographic stability over two centuries. Indeed, the long-term view of population change in Europe is one of *both* growth and decline. Should we view the Holocaust as an exceptional period of demographic decline within an overall stability of European Jewish population size? Should we view the stability of Europe's population as extraordinary, given the losses resulting from the Holocaust and emigration to the United States and Israel? Should we view the two million Jews of Europe today not as representing a decline in numbers but as having been redistributed in new geographic locations from east to west over a period of two centuries? Taking an even longer view, the

total Jewish population of Europe in 1700 was only 719,000. Compara-
tively, the two million Jews living in contemporary Europe represent considerable population growth.

This play with the starting point for demographic comparisons is a
short lesson in how demographic statistics have been used to make an
ideological point. Our thinking is so Holocaust centered that comparisons based on it have become the anchor around which our assessment
of the future revolves. The fragility of our handle on future possibilities
requires us to consider alternative perspectives and different starting
points. Without ignoring the demographic devastation of the Holocaust,
we can assess alternative views and propose new beginnings for evaluating the future of European Jewry. It seems inappropriate to dismiss
the two million Jews living in Europe at the end of the twentieth century and to treat them as vanishing. It appears to me unjustified not only
on simple demographic grounds but also on the basis of the rich history and culture of European Jewish communities and the unique place
of their institutions in the future of world Jewry.

Might it not become a self-fulfilling prophesy to argue that these two
million European Jews are vanishing? Following this logic, the worldwide Jewish community should make minimum investments in Jewish
culture and education for the dying remnants of Europe. Over time, the
result would be that the two million Jews and their descendents would
become weaker in their Jewish commitments and more likely than not
would move toward greater assimilation. In contrast, rethinking Jewish
investment in the future might strengthen the communal basis of that
future in Europe.

The switch from a European-centered Jewish culture to one centered
on the cultures of the United States and Israel came about not only
through the destruction of European Jewry. An equally salient demographic process was immigration. In the period from 1880 to 1920,
some 2.5 million Jews left Europe; 2 million to 3 million more emigrated between 1920 and 1948, and an additional 2.5 million did so in
the last three decades of the twentieth century. Although the comparison is demographic, not moral, the 6 million Jews lost in the Holocaust
were fewer than those lost through immigration. The emphasis on
immigration relates the European demographic decline to the growth

of the Jewish populations of North America, Australia, France, Argentina, and of course Israel. The decline of one Jewish center or core and its replacement by multiple centers were less a matter of erosion and decline than of transformation.

In the last quarter of the twentieth century, the world Jewish population, conservatively estimated, increased by 3 percent. New Jewish communities have emerged as older ones have declined. Sephardic Jewry has experienced a reemergence. Unlike in the past, this segment of world Jewry, with its rich heritage, is no longer silent. It has regained momentum as large numbers of Sephardic immigrants from North Africa have immigrated to France and North America. Ironically, Sephardic Jews from diverse countries of origin have become politically, socially, and culturally articulate in the context of their integration into Israeli society. Ethnic incorporation in Israel (or *klita,* absorption, as used in Hebrew) has often resulted in greater ethnic consciousness.

This brings us to consider not European demography as a whole but the demography of specific parts of Europe where Jewish communal growth is taking place. As in the United States, there is considerable regional and national variation among European Jewish communities, and their futures may not be uniform. Considering this variation, we can assess their future demographic potential as follows. The Jewish communities of France and Great Britain are the largest in western Europe, with estimated populations of 520,000 and 275,000, respectively, at the end of the twentieth century. These two national communities have the greatest potential for continued growth or stability. France has an increasing population of Sephardic Jews, and England has the potential for demographic stability. Both of these communities and other, smaller ones will require new communal leadership and renewed direction to reorganize themselves and emphasize the value of Jewish traditions, history, and culture. As I argue in chapter 6, this demographic potential will require rethinking the place of Jewish values in Jewish culture and transforming the community into an attractive arena of identity for the next generation. The role of Israel should be to reinforce and expand on the new Jewish cultural forms of the transformed communities of Europe. This would require a significant reorientation of Zionist thinking, away from viewing European communities mainly as potential immigrants to Israel or as keepers of the dying legacy of Jewish history.

The Jewish communities of eastern Europe had the largest popula-tions in the past century but suffered the heaviest tolls during the Holocaust and experienced the greatest emigration. Few of these com-munities have been able to recover demographically. As a result of heavy emigration to Israel, the United States, and western Europe, the size of the Jewish population of the former Soviet Union declined from 1.5 mil-lion in 1989 to 500,000 in 2000. Russia had about half of the remain-ing Jewish population of the former Soviet Union in 2000, with significantly larger numbers in the European than in the Asian regions.[11] Although the community in Russia has experienced cultural renewal, the basis of demographic renewal there is less promising. As a result, the 250,000 Jews in Russia are likely to decline further in the next decade. Again, much will depend on the development of Jewish cultural activi-ties and the stability of Russia in general.

Thus, despite aging and communal decline in many areas, and in the face of emigration, major Jewish organizational shifts, and a changing European context, there are significant and large Jewish communities in Europe that have the potential for communal and Jewish cultural renewal and development. Even the Jewish community of Germany has experienced growth and development. In the last quarter of the twenti-eth century, the Jewish population of Germany increased from 30,000 to 70,000, largely through immigration. Germany has the most rapid Jewish population growth in Europe.

From the point of view of Holocaust survivors, their children, and their families, and from the viewpoints of Ashkenazi Jewry and Zionism, Europe's Jewish population has only declined. The religious establish-ment has bemoaned the secularization of European Jewry, particularly in comparison with a romanticized view of religious Jewish communi-ties and institutions of the past. Changing patterns of religion have been interpreted as the end of Jewish distinctiveness. This parallels many people's interpretation of the decline of formal religious activities among American Jews. And from the perspective of rates of intermarriage, the decline looks similar. In reviewing the position of Jews in contempo-rary Europe, Jonathan Webber argues that Jewish communities there are "threatened by one key contemporary phenomenon—intermarriage," which is approaching "crisis proportions." The high rate of marriage between Jews and non-Jews is "the most culturally visible symbol of the dramatic erosion of the Jewish population across Europe."[12] So there is some basis for arguing that European Jewish communities are declining and eroding, if not actually vanishing.

But other trends and new perspectives allow for a different view of the future. There are political, economic, and ethnic trends in the European context, as well as new religious expressions, that are indicative less of erosion than of transformation. These patterns, I argue, take us past the Holocaust and into a new era of relationships between European Jewish communities and the emerging centers of world Jewish life in the United States and Israel. There is evidence for a changing picture of Jewish communities in France and the United Kingdom and in segments of Russia that challenges the doom and gloom assessment of Europe's Jewish future.

It seems to me that the end of European hegemony over world politics and economy finds its parallel in the Jewish communities there. No one seriously argues that Europe's fall from dominance will result in the erosion of European society or the end of the vitality of European life. Rather, the change is seen as one of transformation from a situation of dominance to one in which Europe takes its place in a new global society. Surely Europe (read also Jewish communities) has changed in dramatic ways. But it would be an error to view the ascendance of non-European countries as eliminating western European culture or politics or economy. Most would agree that the European stage has changed or been transformed. So it is with European Jews. Viewing Jews in the context of these broader issues remains the essential message.

ISRAEL'S JEWISH DEMOGRAPHIC SURVIVAL

What about the Jewish community of Israel—the "dawn of Jewish redemption"? Is Israel the anchor of the Jewish future? Those concerned about the decline and erosion of Jewish communities in the European and American "Diaspora" view Israel as the major or the demographic hope for the future. "Israel's future is no longer in doubt," argues Bernard

Wasserstein, along with many others.[13] And the evidence from demography seems to support that view.[14]

The Jewish population in Israel has increased dramatically over the last several decades, not least because of the immigration to Israel of millions of European Jews. It has continued to grow through immigration and through a trend toward somewhat larger family size than has been observed among Jews elsewhere. Demographically, the story of the Israeli Jewish community is one of growth and a relatively young age distribution, compared with the very slow growth of the American Jewish population and with the population decline and aging of some major Jewish communities in Europe. The prospects for Israel's becoming the demographic center of world Jewry seem clear on the horizon. Because Jewish losses in Israel due to assimilation through intermarriage are minimal, the logic of the future demography of Israel's Jewish community appears incontrovertible.

Jews in Israel marry other Jews, value the Jewish family highly, and almost universally celebrate Jewish national holidays and are committed to Jewish nationalism. They observe Saturday as the Jewish Sabbath, speak a Jewish language, and are close to Jewish cultural forms. So marriage, Jewish networks, Jewish public ritual observances, and ethnic or national Jewishness flourish in a country where more than 80 percent of the population is Jewish. Social interaction, family relations, work relationships with other Jews, Jewish political control, and socialization in Jewish schools and the military, along with cohesion induced by external pressures and reinforced by continuing Jewish immigration, make Israel the new Jewish "shtetl." In its cohesion, Israel is similar to eastern European communities of the past, where Jewishness (then defined as Yiddishkeit) flourished. But Israel is different from the former shtetl communities in its national character, its political control, the majority demographic status of its Jews, its economic development, and its religious autonomy. Only in their demographic growth, communal cohesion, and Judaic character are Jews in Israel similar to those of the shtetl communities of the past.

Israel is the quintessential contemporary Jewish community, with high levels of national cohesion. Even the perpetuation of ethnic Jewish communities within Israel and its division by social class, immigrant status, gender, region, and religious activities do not conflict with the demographic and social viability of Israeli Jewish society.[15]

Do these internal and external forces ensure the quality of Jewish life in the State of Israel? What are the indicators of Jewish quality among those living in a Jewish state? What about Judaism in Israel and the Jewish values of justice and equality? Do these apply to the minority of Arabs living in Israel, or to Jewish women? The answers to these questions are less certain. The evidence for socioeconomic inequalities in Israel is powerful, as is the evidence for discrimination against women and minorities. Ugly cultural wars are taking place between religious Jews and secular Israelis, and political corruption extends to the very top of the political and religious elite. The demographic viability of a Jewish community may be one basis for thinking about its future, and perhaps a necessary condition for its continuity. But having a demographic base does not necessarily ensure the quality of Jewish life.

Certainly the vision that some founders of the State of Israel had of a Jewish society that would be a "light unto the nations" had been redefined by the end of the twentieth century. It is hard to reconcile Jewish quality of life in Israel with the large number of non-Jewish guest workers from Romania, the Philippines, and Thailand and with the observation that half of the Russian immigrants entering Israel in 1999 and 2000 under the "law of return" were not Jewish but members of extended Jewish families. When one sees political corruption, economic wars and competition, socioeconomic and ethnic inequalities, religious and cultural battles, and Mafia-like activities among leaders, it is difficult to share the enthusiasm David Ben Gurion expressed when he saw a prostitute in Tel Aviv as a symbol of Jewish societal "normalcy" and recited the prayer, "Thank God I lived and survived to this day."

I concluded from the quantitative evidence about Jews in the United States and Europe that the fundamental issue for the Jewish future is the quality of Jewish life. I shall raise the quality question about Jewish culture in Israel again in chapter 6. The quality of Jewish life obviously varies in different national and community contexts. We need to address the elements of this quality that characterize different parts of world Jewry as a basis for assessing the future of the Jews.

CONCLUDING THOUGHTS

Jews today are different from previous generations of Jews; the nostal-
gia of the past enriches the present, but the contexts of Jews' lives are
very different. Just as today's Jews are uncomfortable with the Judaism,
Jewish institutions, and Jewish culture of their grandparents, so are their
grandchildren unlikely to feel comfortable with their own grandparents'
religion, institutions, and culture—for they, too, will face a new, transformed world. Indeed, the challenge for the contemporary Jewish community is to draw on the rich legacies of the past in order to prepare for
the unknowns of the future. We cannot know the future, but Jews can
learn and teach a range of options and values that may serve as guidelines. As their children and grandchildren build new forms of Jewish
expression to meet their needs, the major challenge is to have the vision
to incorporate their worlds into that of their parents and grandparents
and to link the present world to theirs in new ways. Quantitative issues
will surely play a necessary but not a sufficient role in the creative futures
of Jewish communities.

The next generation is unlikely to be the last generation of Jews. Elder
Jews today should see to that, as their parents saw to it that the present
generation was not the last. Jews need to teach about the past through
the eyes of the present, to study their distinctiveness in new and creative ways in order to guide the future. They need new vision to adjust
to the new realities of the twenty-first century. The changes demand not
the magic to re-create the benefits of the past without its costs, but the
power of concerted community activities that involve all Jews in the totality of their lives. Jewish strength lies in Jewish institutions and community networks. Jews have a powerful community, one linked to their
past and their people. They need to find a way to attract the next generation to Jewish history and quality of life, even as they struggle to help
the current generation redefine its attachments to Judaism and Jewishness. Jews need to extend their hands to others, even as they focus primarily on themselves.

The American Jewish community and communities in parts of
Europe and Israel have become strong in some ways and weak in others. Jews do not live in ideal communities; they never have. The goal is

to build on the communities' strengths, not to bemoan their weaknesses. Instead of asking of the numbers whether they show that Jews are surviving, let us apply the data to address the question, Survival for what? How do we enhance the quality of Jewish life through institutions and social-cultural networks? I address the question of the quality of Jewish life in the following chapters. The message in this review is that much needs to be done to ensure that the Jewish community of the future will be a worthwhile one, so that those who have choices in the next generation will choose it. And there is a solid demographic base for assuming that there will be Jews in key communities around the world to make those choices.

In the past, Jews had little choice. Constrained by the environment and by fear, they had little vision of what could be, because they knew little of what was. Today, Jews have an exceptionally wide range of choices. As a Jew, I would urge that we need to make those choices with the past as our guide but also with a vision of future possibilities, with experience as our history but not as our constraint. Let us begin to build constructively on the strengths we have in order to meet the challenges of the future.

3

FORECASTING JEWISH POPULATIONS

Forecasting, or projecting, populations has been one of the ways in which social scientists have studied futures. Using detailed quantitative evidence and what appear to be sound statistical data, the population expert portrays the future in "objective" empirical form. The resulting statistical figures are impressive for most nondemographers, reinforcing their expectations about the future and confirming their interpretations. Rarely are population forecasts used to reject preconceived views of the future. The projected population numbers often take on the aura of scientific certainty and inevitability. Demographers' cautions and qualifications are lost in the details of the text or buried in appendices and footnotes that are rarely acknowledged or read. The *use* of population projections is driven less by demographic science than by ideology or theory.

Demographers regularly acknowledge the limitations of the baseline evidence they use and recognize the need for multiple population projections in their calculations. But the voices of caution and modesty are not heard when ideological imperatives or policy commitments take precedence. Users and interpreters of population projections have been guilty of exaggerating the objective bases of estimates of future population patterns and, even more seriously, of building communal policy on weak demographic foundations. Policy planning is not guided by multiple forecasts. Proponents of ideologies about the future are not interested in probabilities. By exposing the ideological foundations of population projections, my goal is to establish the context for thinking through alternative Jewish demographic futures. In this chapter I reexamine the issues of Jewish futures through the prism of population projections.

The demographic or quantitative arguments that have been made in predicting the decline, erosion, or disappearance of some Jewish communities have been based on assumptions about present patterns and their future trajectories. The predictions have been derived from estimated communal statistical portraits couched in the language of demographic science. I argued in the previous chapter that an evaluation of the whole array of available evidence, including demographic analysis, lends no support to the conclusion of future Jewish communal dissolution in the United States, Israel, and several countries of Europe. I develop my argument further in this chapter by turning to a direct assessment of Jewish population projections in order to reveal their limitations for studying the future.

The value of any population projection is based on three features: the baseline estimates of the population's size and characteristics; the quality of information about factors that will influence future population changes; and the assumptions made about future changes in the processes that shape the sizes and compositions of populations. In the demography of contemporary Jewish communities, all three of these features are weak, and estimates and projections are often made on the basis of poor-quality data. When these weaknesses are combined with other limitations of population projections for small, minority subpopulations, the result is that estimates of the future size and characteristics of the Jewish population are severely limited. Population projections should be viewed as a basis for assessing the implications of short-term *extensions* of current patterns. Only rarely have Jewish population projections taken into account future changes in the directions of population processes. Therefore, the results of any exercise in projecting the population for purposes of assessing the future should be interpreted cautiously and critically. All population projections are limited, and most of the limitations are applicable to Jewish population projections. But projections of the Jewish population have additional limitations, which I shall identify.

I start with a review of the major set of Jewish population projections that has been the basis of much discussion and planning in the Jewish community. I show how these projections are based on a limited and problematic series of assumptions about the future (and the past). I then turn to comparisons with general population projections, identifying some of their theoretical and methodological assumptions and how they are helpful in evaluating Jewish population projections. It will become clear that estimates of the consequences of marriage, family formation, and fertility among Jews have been used to predict a future crisis of Jewish demographic growth in some Jewish communities. These predictions often include assessments of the negative demographic implications of high rates of intermarriage. The appearance of scientific accuracy and the intimidation people often feel in the face of statistical evidence have led to powerful but unwarranted negative conclusions about Jewish futures.

My goal is to demystify for the nondemographer the fundamentals of Jewish population projections without the technical or statistical details.[1] I want to empower the generalist to detect some of the underlying assumptions and themes of population forecasting. I do not dispute the bases of the statistical calculations used to arrive at population projections, but I challenge some of the logic underlying the projections and the selective future population scenarios that have been presented. For this exercise there is no need to present alternative statistical projections, because a careful reading of the existing range of projections provides ample support for an alternative, more positive assessment of Jewish demographic futures.

Based on a review of general and Jewish population projections, I have reached three broad conclusions. First, there is nothing inevitable about future Jewish demographic trends. Very few conclusions can be drawn about potential population changes in the next generation. Most importantly, available population projections do not convincingly reveal the range of future possibilities of Jewish communal developments. At best, they represent an assessment of the implications of current patterns, but they do not serve as a programmed basis for exploring changes in the future.

Second, current forecasting of Jewish population trends is based on assumptions about the future that are not consistent with complete or systematic social science evidence. Alternative premises about demographic and social processes would result in very different population projections.

And third, existing Jewish population projections point to equally plausible scenarios that are significantly different from current assessments of Jewish futures based on these projections. The major problem with population projections is their interpretation, not their statistical design, although there are grounds for questioning their statistical assumptions and the limited range of future changes that is often presented.

To support my conclusions, I review the most widely cited and most elaborate set of Jewish demographic projections and their underlying assumptions. Most of their inferences and conclusions beyond the short run of two decades appear to me to be baseless. Sometimes, when current patterns are extended over several generations, the demographic implications are absurd. These longer-term population projections have been picked up by Jewish journalists and reprinted in the popular press as part of the alarmist position of those who deny the continuity of Jewish communities outside of Israel. They have also been used to reinforce political views about the deteriorating ratio of Jewish to Arab population size in Israel. The views of Diaspora Jewish communal erosion and the demographic danger to Jewish dominance in Israel are, I believe, misguided and distorted. They are derived from flawed past research and distorting population forecasts.

JEWISH POPULATION FORECASTS AND PROJECTIONS: A CONTEMPORARY ILLUSTRATION

A set of Jewish population projections has been prepared under the auspices of the Institute of Contemporary Jewry at the Hebrew University of Jerusalem. These projections and variants of them have been widely published in Jewish yearbooks and in Jewish forums over the last several decades. The projections have been revised and refined in their most recent presentations, published between 2000 and 2002, but their themes are continuous with those of previous projections.[2] All of them make a series of limited assumptions about future Jewish demographic changes. They extend the current estimated populations for dozens of Jewish communities for a long period of time. The various projections incorporate minimal changes in current rates of growth and in the processes associated with family formation, family structure, inter-marriage, and migration. Hence, their assumptions ensure that pro-jections for several decades into the future predict inevitable population decline for Jewish communities outside the State of Israel.

The projections are complex and meticulously prepared. The difficul-ties associated with projecting Jewish populations are noted, along with multiple variants of future population size and composition. Indeed, a density of qualifications and cautions is presented. No one knows the limitations of these projections better than do their authors. Yet most of the detailed statistics presented about the future are selective of a nar-row range of possibilities that fall within a predetermined framework. The conclusions drawn and the interpretations given convey an ideo-logical message couched in the science of numbers and wrapped in the details of statistical presentation. I reach different conclusions as I review these projections and interpret their implications.

How are these Jewish population projections organized and presented? They usually start with the estimated Jewish population size in 1945, a low point in recent Jewish demographic history. That date is also just prior to the establishment of the State of Israel and mass migration to it in 1948–51. Between 1945 and 2000, the total Diaspora Jewish pop-ulation was reduced by an estimated 2 million persons (from 10.4 mil-lion to 8.3 million). Almost the entire decline—99 percent—was due to migration and population redistribution. These data reveal the shift away from the European concentration of Jewish population through large-scale immigration to Israel, North America, and South Africa. It is a descriptive picture of post-World War II Jewish population redistri-bution: some Jewish communities decline as others expand. It can hardly be called a picture of the disintegration and erosion of world Jewry.

Building on data from 1945 to the 1990s, the newer projections begin with the year 2000 and end in 2080. In publishing their projections, the researchers appropriately emphasize the period 2000–2030. The longer-range projections are there to "illustrate the nature of possible change in the longer term, namely, new developments that might emerge given prolonged extension of current trends." Extending current trends for eight decades, from 2000 to 2080, cannot be the basis for policy planning. No one, not even the researchers who prepared these projections, argues for their predictive value. Their authors recognize that any error made in an earlier decade or two will have major demographic consequences in later decades, as errors and misjudgments cumulate. They acknowledge that although the projections are organized to follow "a linear path," Jewish history itself has not followed such a straight-line course.

Underlying the shape of the projections is a twofold argument that is cautiously but relentlessly presented. First, there are the inevitable declines in what are referred to as Diaspora Jewish populations—those Jewish communities outside the State of Israel. Second, future reductions in the sizes of Jewish communities outside of Israel are contrasted with the growth of the Israeli Jewish population. Together these points lead to a calculation of the increasing proportion of world Jewry that will be located in Israel. The ideological message is not obscured in either the projections or the authors' interpretation: Jews living outside of Israel have a weak demographic future. Only in Israel is there a basis for Jewish demographic growth and survival. As Jewish communities decline and "erode" in the Diaspora, the Jewish population of Israel is projected to show "a continuing trend of substantial growth." In comparing the two main Jewish demographic centers, Israel and the United States, the argument is almost always one of future Jewish population decline in the United States versus increase in Israel.

The potential inclusion of significant numbers of the non-Jewish members of Jewish households in Israel (primarily those who arrived as members of Jewish households in the recent immigration from the former Soviet Union) would further increase the growth of the Israeli Jewish population. Reluctantly noted is the possibility of a similar pattern of non-Jewish-born members of Jewish households in communities outside of Israel. In limiting the projections to "core" Jewish households, these people are specifically removed from calculations of future Jewish populations in Diaspora communities. The number of potential non-Jewish members of Jewish households in Israel is relatively small and inconsequential, whereas the number in the United States would be large.

Their inclusion as part of the Jewish population of the United States would significantly change the population projections and would more closely reflect the reality of those people's Jewish commitments.

The projections appropriately disentangle the various components of population and focus on the demographic implications of current low levels of Jewish fertility in Diaspora countries. It is recognized that migration between countries where Jewish populations reside is the most powerful potential source of change and variation in the future. Nevertheless, it is difficult to project multiple migration possibilities over an eighty-year period, and therefore few migration projections are presented.

In making their forecasts for North America and some western European countries, the authors of these projections used as their estimated future fertility rate the "current" rate for those nations.[3] That is, fertility is estimated at 1.5 children per woman (the current estimated total fertility rate in the cross section), with a range of 1.1 to 1.9—that is, plus or minus 0.4. Most of the data and the discussion are presented for the "medium level," which, at 1.5, is a low estimate for at least some of the major Jewish communities. For example, the medium estimate of the fertility rate for the Jewish population in the United States is assumed to be 1.5 over the entire eighty-year period. There are indications, however, that this cross-sectional rate reflects the timing of marriage and childbearing in the U.S. at the present time and that average completed family size is in fact likely to be closer to 2.0 than to 1.5 (see note 3). The United States in general had already moved toward an estimated 2.1 lifetime family size in 2002.[4] Early results from the 2000 National Jewish Population Survey in the United States included an estimate of completed family size (for the older cohort of women, ages 40–44) of 1.8 children. The argument has often been made that Jews have been in the forefront of demographic change, and that has been applied to the decline in fertility in the nineteenth century and to the postwar baby boom in Western countries. It perhaps should also be applied to estimates of completed family size when fertility fluctuates around lower levels. Hence, the upper level of fertility, estimated at 1.9 children per woman, may be closer to the future fertility rate for Jews in North America generally and in the United States particularly.[5]

The inevitable result when Jewish populations are projected at "medium" levels of fertility (1.5 children per woman in North America and 2.5 in Israel, the current fertility rate for that country) for eighty years is a decline of Jewish populations outside of Israel and an increase within Israel. Even the low rate for North America, however, yields remarkable overall population stability there for the twenty years up to 2020. The major population decline under this fertility assumption occurs between 2050 and 2080. A higher, and I would argue a more realistic, estimate of long-term fertility (a total fertility of 1.9) would result in Jewish population stability in North America through 2080. Yet the authors refer to the "significant demographic erosion" that will affect North American Jewry after the year 2030.

The decline in Diaspora Jewish populations forecast by members of the Institute of Contemporary Jewry is largely a European phenomenon. At a projected fertility level of 1.5 for segments of western European Jewish populations, and at a significantly lower level (1.1) for most of eastern Europe, the European Jewish population will decline and age. Nevertheless, even under these minimum demographic circumstances, the size of the European Jewish population is likely to be around 1 million by 2030. Jewish population size in Europe is retained even with an estimated decline in the Jewish population of the former Soviet Union from 413,000 in 2000 to 22,000 in 2030 and 0 in 2080. This projection is based on a continuation of the rate of emigration seen in the early 1990s. One difficulty in forecasting many European Jewish populations over the long term is that of estimating international migration and using the cross-sectional figure for current fertility of 1.1 as the basis for estimating eventual family size. Those who do not foresee the total emptying out of the former Soviet Union by way of continuous emigration will arrive at a very different regional future for European Jewry.

The overriding issue in many Jewish communities in Europe (and for European populations in general) is the aging trend that follows from low fertility and low mortality. Low fertility and the aging of the European population in general have been driving forces in encouraging international labor migration to European countries. That has been a positive source of growth for many Jewish communities outside of Israel—those in the United States, Canada, France, and, most recently, Germany—

but aging is likely to have negative demographic consequences for many European Jewish communities.

PROJECTING JEWISH FAMILY FORMATION

One difficult issue that remains unresolved is the future rate of family formation among Jews. The use of cross-sectional estimates (how many persons are currently married) rather than life course trends (how many persons eventually marry) for projecting marriage patterns into the future, even more than the use of such estimates for fertility, borders on the absurd. In one set of projections from the Institute of Contemporary Jewry, current marriage rates are extended without change into the future. One of the authors of the projections, Sergio DellaPergola, writes that "if current behaviors continue, about 40–50 per cent of the young adult generation in western countries will never marry. . . . it is not surprising to find that Jewish populations [in those countries are] moving in the same direction"—that is, the direction of nonmarriage.[6] Of course we do not know the future rate of marriage and family formation among Jews or others, but it is highly unlikely that current patterns, measured on the basis of a cross section that includes many people who have delayed marriage but who will marry when they are older, will continue over an extended period of time. Cross sections do not reflect longer-term trends when changes are occurring throughout the life course. Certainly the proportion of people not marrying has increased in North America and western Europe in the last several decades, but the 40–50 percent estimate of the currently unmarried is largely a reflection of timing. Marriage postponed is not marriage foregone for Jewish young adults over the next several decades.

Future fertility assumptions depend not only on the unknown future sizes of Jewish families but also on the future family sizes of those who intermarry with persons not born Jewish. Thus, the impact of fertility assumptions is greater than the impact of international migration, because those assumptions incorporate the "patterns of identification of children born to out-married Jewish parents." The issue is, What happens to population projections when social scientists eliminate children from the core Jewish population because one of the parents is identified as not being Jewish?

One study followed up on families identified as intermarried in the United States National Jewish Population Study of 1990.[7] The conclusion was that large numbers of adult children of intermarriages still identified themselves as ethnic Jews even though in "religious terms they define themselves as non-Jewish." The research showed the coexistence of Jewish and Christian religious rituals in such families. Both the Jewish and the non-Jewish partner wanted to pass something on to their children. Judging from these data, it is inappropriate to eliminate the children of the intermarried from future population projections.

The evidence from the 1990 United States National Jewish Population Survey was that among all mixed marriages (when the non-Jewish-born person was not converted to Judaism), 18 percent of the children living at home were being raised as Jewish, 25 percent as both Jewish and Christian, 33 percent as Christian, and 24 percent as having no religion. These data have been widely interpreted as representing a loss to the Jewish community of all those who were not being raised solely as Jews. Hence, projections treat almost all the children of mixed marriages as non-Jewish. My interpretation takes the counterview. I argue that only one-third of mixed-marriage families are raising their children as Christians. Hence, all others might contribute to the future population of Jews. Surely the "true" projection lies somewhere in the middle. Children of mixed marriages represent potential Jewish demographic stability and perhaps demographic gains.[8]

JEWISH AND ARAB
POPULATION PROJECTIONS IN ISRAEL

In the published projections under discussion, the emphasis on the decline of Jewish communities in the Diaspora is matched by another concern about the Jewish population in Israel: that the Jewish majority has a lower rate of population growth than the Arab minority. I turn briefly to this side issue because it is central to the theory behind the population projections. The issue has a long history, which I have outlined elsewhere.[9] I note here that the Jewish population of Israel has retained, at a fairly constant ratio, an overwhelming demographic majority relative to Arab Israelis since the establishment of the state. The demo-

graphic "threat" of Arab growth rates in Israel is a powerful myth emphasized by Israel-centered theories of Jewish community life and nationalist fear of Arabs, but it has little basis in Israel's demographic reality.

In one set of projections, the Arab Palestinian population includes
not only the Arabs living inside Israel but also those in the West Bank
and Gaza, about 3 million persons in 2000. The goal is to show the "dan-
gers" to Jewish population hegemony if the current differential growth
rates continue until 2080. The resulting population projections are
indeed absurd. With unchanged fertility, the total population of Arab
Palestinians, both inside Israel and in the West Bank and Gaza, would
grow to 6.6 million in 2020 and 22 million in 2050. The authors themselves state that these scenarios "defy imagination" and cannot be taken
as "realistic." And of course Palestinians living in the West Bank and
Gaza are not part of the State of Israel. Within the boundaries of the
state, no demographic scenario envisions a loss of a Jewish majority in
the next many decades.

The Israel-centered theory of Jewish demographic history and of future
demography forecasts a twofold trend: the potential end of Jewish communities outside of Israel and an increasingly threatened Jewish demographic position inside the country. This is an odd set of conclusions
for a thoughtful demographic exercise. It is illustrative of population forecasting gone awry into long-term prediction. The elementary but major
scientific lesson of these projections is not about the inevitable decline
of Diaspora Jewish populations or the "momentum of demographic
mechanisms." It is certainly not a lesson on assumptions about the continuation of demographic rates into the longer-term future. Nor is it about
the inherent danger of Palestinian population growth to the Jewish State
of Israel. The lesson to be learned is that there are analytic costs when
ideological biases lead one to project unchanging, straight-line population processes into the distant future.

GENERAL ISSUES IN POPULATION PROJECTIONS

The limitations of Jewish population projections derive in part from some
general problems associated with all projections. I briefly review these
general issues in order to further assess the specifics of the Jewish case.

The first major attempts at systematic population projections were made in the late nineteenth century. These were largely linear projections, that is, starting with current estimates of population growth and statistically extending the patterns into the future. These linear projections were often based on preconceived "natural laws" of population growth. Most were carried out by statisticians who were fascinated by the increase (or decrease) of the population predicted through the extension of trend lines. In the 1920s, linear extrapolations gave way to more complex thinking about possible natural laws of population growth. But the newer efforts, too, were statistical exercises, ignoring social, political, and cultural upheavals. Extrapolations from the present population pattern to estimate the "inevitable" trajectory of population growth in the future were a favorite exercise among some of the early demographers. Often these statistical exercises were useful only in assessing the implications of current growth rather than predicting future possibilities.

When demographers extricated themselves from the natural science mode to enter the world of social science after World War II, they moved away from statistical inevitability and natural laws. They referred to "forecasting" rather than "projecting," or extrapolating population trends for prediction. Forecasting involved two additions to projecting: incorporating a wider range of variables than the strictly demographic in estimating future population and using the language of estimation and probabilities, not that of laws.[10]

Instead of making one set of projections, demographers now specified a range of possible futures, entering diverse factors into their equations and creating alternative scenarios. Eventually, they began to make short-term forecasts through complex and multiple pathways, starting from the past and working through the present to the future. Nevertheless, such general population forecasts always involve three problem areas. First and foremost is the inability to predict disruptions of current demographic trends. Population projections deal in large part with the demographic consequences of present trends and their extension into the future. When a population is growing, then projections will extend the growth; when they are declining, the trend line of decline will be continued. At best, trend lines might be modified to generate a level of population stability. Although projections can shift from growth or decline to stability, changes in direction are almost never projected or forecast. Few demographers have incorporated the effects of wars or disasters in their predictions of the future, and fewer still have forecast baby booms or busts, new types of family formations, or new directions of internal migration.

A second, relatively minor problem in forecasting is the selection of the starting point for the time series. When should the trend line begin, especially if there have been historical zigs and zags of population changes? In projecting the population of the United States, for example, should one start with the baby boom of the 1950s or the baby bust of the 1970s? Should one begin with the new immigration patterns of the late 1960s and the 1970s or with the sharper increase in the 1980s and 1990s? How does one decide whether or not a population forecast should incorporate the later marriage and cohabitation patterns of the 1990s and their impact on the timing of childbearing, or the divorce and remarriage trends that started in the 1960s? Moreover, how long should one make the intervals over which estimates will be forecast?

A third problem in population projections is deciding how far trends should be projected into the future. The major guess is when the open interval of the present patterns should be closed. On what basis does one decide whether the observed pattern is the beginning, the middle, or the end of a trend? Most population extensions used for policy purposes are limited to the short run, around ten or twenty years. The longer the predictions in time, the more likely unpredicted events and disruptions in population processes will occur.

Authors of population projections tend to employ the so-called *ceteris parabis* principle—the assumption that all other things, the nondemographic parameters, will remain the same. Unfortunately, the reverse assumption, that all other things will change, is more characteristic of modern societies in both the long and the short runs. Population projections carry through the logic of present and immediate past demographic trends to extend them into the near future. The longer in time the prediction, the more likely it is that unpredicted events will get in the way of accuracy. In general, demographers argue that population forecasts should be made for horizons no longer than thirty years or so, and they suggest that different methods of forecasting and of assessing uncertainty are appropriate in different time horizons.[11] Population projections that extend into the next generation, beyond what may be considered the short run, are most unlikely to be accurate predictions of the future. Projections that are two or more generations in the future are mostly guesses and often demographic fantasies. A review of published projections suggests the principle that "the potential for error in population projections rises with the length of the projection interval." Beyond one or two decades into the future, "uncertainty accumulates rapidly and nonlinearly." This is the so-called length effect, or the loss of precision as projection time lengthens.[12] Uncertainty arises both because the present demographic situation is not known perfectly and because future trends in population components are subject to unpredictable influences.

Thus, the projection of current population patterns reveals what is likely to happen to the population *if nothing changes*. Projections are powerful indicators of what the contours of a population will look like if current rates continue, and they are insightful as commentaries on the present demographic profile. Often, projections signal to policy makers the need to take action to limit the consequences of current population patterns. Ironically, population projections are best understood as policy tools that can help ensure that the predicted outcomes will *not* come about, especially if these have negative consequences. The most helpful population projections from a policy point of view are those that are least successful from the perspective of demographic prediction.

PROJECTING POPULATION COMPONENTS

Most attempts at population forecasts have been based on theories about the ways in which one of the components of population changes or remains stable. Age variation in population processes is most often used as the basis for predicting futures, with the assumption that the older ages can be used as the basis for suggesting what the characteristics of the younger age groups will be when they age. As the older ages are the indicators of what was, so the younger ages are what will be. Of course this is only the case when age-specific rates remain the same. In reality, this is the most unlikely scenario for the future in the modern period, because age-specific stability is the least likely pattern.[13]

Population projections reflect a complex combination of estimates of the future of the demographic processes that shape population size. There are three components of population change—fertility, mortality, and migration. Each of these is a fundamental element of the population system, in the sense that any change in population size must reflect some combination of changes in the three. Any factor that is considered directly or indirectly to influence population size and structure operates only through the processes of fertility, mortality, and migration. To complicate matters, each of the processes has somewhat different determinants and trajectories, and each has a profound but variable relationship with the other two, independently of, as well as in conjunction with, its relationship to population growth.

Many projections treat the population as "closed"—that is, closed to migration in or out. This assumption means one has only to project the future course of fertility and mortality. As a result, the need to deal with the greater uncertainties and volatility of internal migration for local populations and international migration for national populations is eliminated. In the recent period, the assumption of a closed population has become more problematic as the migration factor has become more important both within and between countries.

Forecasts that focus solely on fertility and mortality often treat population as a "natural" process, given the biological aspects of fertility and mortality, in contrast to migration. Projection of the "biological" processes of reproduction and death tends to de-emphasize the need to consider the social components involved. By definition, population forecasts have become poor predictors of population changes due to migration. The larger the effects of migration on population change, the less valuable the forecasts based solely on fertility and mortality. The smaller the unit for which population projections are made, the greater the impact of migration. International migration is the most difficult component to predict, partly because it is the result of complex processes of policy development and enforcement in the sending and receiving countries. And because of the unpredictability of internal migration, it is always more difficult to project the future populations of local areas than of nations, and of immigrant populations than of the native born.

The mortality processes underlying population projections tend to be more straightforward, because mortality rates change relatively slowly and usually without major disruptions, except in the case of wars or natural disasters. As in other cases of disruptions, the demographic results of mortality disruptions are difficult to include in population projections. Omitting such unpredictable mortality events ruins the accuracy of population projections in some contexts. However, the major emphasis of population forecasting has been on the future of fertility. Indeed, most population forecasts have become focused primarily on the fertility component, and thus population projections tend largely to be projections of fertility trends. Fertility projections tend to show the future implications of current fertility, assuming either the continuation of trends (whether the high fertility rates of third world countries or the low fertility rates of Western countries) or a move toward stability. Demographers have not been very accurate in dealing with unpredictable shifts from fertility declines to baby booms to stability or with shifts in the timing of childbearing.

What has been the experience of demographers when they have constructed fertility projections? In the 1930s, a series of population projections was constructed for the United States on the basis of cross-sectional accounts of fertility. These projections were made at a time of serious restrictions on immigration to the United States and so were based on assumptions of a closed population. The future fertility estimates predicted a maximum population of 180 million by 1980, followed by a continuous decline based on the low rate of fertility observed during the economic depression of the 1930s. Not surprisingly, at least in retrospect, the forecast of the "inevitable" decline of the U.S. population due to below-replacement-level fertility was inaccurate. The authors of the projections were unable to foresee the power of the baby boom and subsequent fertility fluctuations (not to mention the fluctuations of migration to and from the United States), which made the 1980 U.S. population closer to 250 million.

There are no grounds for projecting continuous population decline (or continuous growth) solely on the basis of past snapshots of the cross section. Fertility was a variable that changed over the life courses of families and in response to economic, political, social, and familial contexts. Fluctuations in both the timing of childbearing and in the sizes of completed families needed to be incorporated into the projections of population. Annual fertility rates were to be taken not as the whims and fashions of people making casual decisions but rather as reflections of behavior embedded in the social and economic contexts of their lives.

Little can be known with confidence about the future fertility levels of a population. Variation in fertility is unlikely to be dramatic; in the United States, a generational change of at most one child per family has been documented. Indeed, a recent U.S. National Academy of Sciences report notes that "once low fertility levels are reached, further fertility change is largely indeterminate. For any given date in the future, fertility levels are quite unpredictable and substantial variability is likely." With regard to future fertility, the report continues, ultimate or long-term levels "are unlikely to be either well above, or well below, two children per woman."[14] Even relatively small changes in the timing of childbearing and the fertility rate can have significant implications for population growth and structure. As more families are able to control the timing of their childbearing and the number of children they have, the more likely it is that such decisions will fluctuate in response to external as well as family issues.

Most fertility projections assume the stability of the family unit as currently constructed. In fact, family units are changing—dissolving and recombining—and so the family stability assumptions underlying fertility projections become problematic. For example, many couples in which one or both partners have had previous marriages go on to have additional children, especially if one member of the newly formed couple is childless. The effects of such fluctuations and recombinations are multiplied for smaller populations. Most importantly, the projection of future fertility patterns becomes inextricably intertwined with the forecasting of changes in family structure and family formation. These have become another set of complicating factors in population projections as new family forms have emerged.[15] These new forms, including cohabitation, delayed marriage, postponed childbearing, and remarriage, are intimately linked to changing education and economic opportunities for men and women. As a result, it has become clear that traditional methods of population projection that focus solely on demographic processes without forecasting the changing links between education, economic opportunity, and family formation will fail to capture the complexities of future fertility changes. Projections that do not include the changing structure of families will likely miss the mark.[16]

PROJECTING JEWISH POPULATION SIZE

Essentially, projecting population size and structure is a matter of dealing with "entering" and "exiting" processes—that is, how people enter or leave the population.[17] This approach is appropriate for entire national populations but not for minority ones, for which entering and exiting can occur in ways other than through birth, death, or movement. Some populations can be entered or exited through personal identification, formal membership, or religious conversion. Projections of such populations require attention to additional processes that are much more complex to estimate. This requirement is of particular importance for assessing Jewish population projections.

In general, population projections for ethnic or religious minorities are significantly more complicated than those for national populations. First, basic data on minority populations are often less accurate than data for the population as a whole. The quality of any population projection is never greater than the quality of the basic observable data. Often there are poor baseline data and only estimates of the fundamental components of the population. When census data are unavailable or incomplete, demographers have gathered survey data instead. These have been used in innovative ways to estimate future fertility by investigating family size plans, expectations, and ideals.[18] Without major disruptions over the life course or changes in the norms of fertility, individual-level expectations offer a better basis for studying future family size than does merely extrapolating from past trends.[19] The dependence of Jewish population projections on surveys for data on baseline behavior and expectations make this innovation particularly important.

A second complication is the role of international and local population movements, which often loom larger for minority populations than for majority ones. When ethnic populations are residentially concentrated, population projections become more complex.

A third set of issues in minority population projections relates to processes that affect population size beyond the standard demographic exiting and entering. These include changing forms of identification among minority group members and the broader definitional question of who is included in the group. There may be population gains and losses through new forms of identity at the individual level, in addition to the effects of births, deaths, and migration, and changes in the categorical inclusion of members within the minority population. Hence, projecting the populations of such groups is complicated by changes in the populations that should be compared over time.[20] And for some populations that are defined in part by religious identification, no data are obtained in the official national censuses of many countries, including the United States. Nor are reliable national data available on additions and subtractions through conversion, life course events, and changes in the ways persons identify themselves.

Taken together, these general considerations suggest that the potential value of forecasting future Jewish population changes is extremely limited. I draw four primary conclusions. First, population projections for Jewish communities are seriously constrained by the absence of baseline data on current religious identification in many censuses. Basing population projections on sample surveys raises important questions about coverage and definitions, particularly questions about which Jews were included in the survey and how they were defined. The absence of national longitudinal survey data on Jews limits population projections to cross-sectional survey data.

Second, the diverse ways of expressing Jewish identification and their fluctuations over time and over the life course force us to measure and estimate changes in identification as the life course unfolds and between generations. Projections based on measures of identification at one point in time are unlikely to capture the depth or diversity of Jewish identification no matter how detailed the measures may be. This limitation is a central concern in the analysis of *demographic* changes (and projections), not only in the study of shifts in ethnic and religious identification in their own right.

Third, in projecting Jewish population growth and structure it is necessary to focus on changes brought about by both internal and international migration. The inclusion of these processes is essential, given the experiences of Jewish communities in the past century.

Fourth, the centrality of family formation and family structural changes for projecting the future of a small and dispersed minority population requires that family-related processes among Jews be treated systematically as life course variables. Yet changes in these family-related processes are particularly difficult to project into the future. The changing identification of Jews over the life course makes estimation of the future of Jewish intermarriage for Jewish population changes most problematic.

These constraints and limitations are critical cautions for our understanding of Jewish population projections and their accuracy. Why then are such projections carried out? Some of them serve obvious short-term goals such as Jewish community planning. These have little analytic interest. Others have been used to understand the implications of the continuation of present patterns. A major conclusion of my general review of population projections is that studying projections of Jewish populations reveals more about conceptions of the present Jewish community than about what is likely to happen in the future. In this regard, forecasts of Jewish demographic erosion reflect an *ideology* of communal decline rather than the inevitable results of statistical analysis.

The record of accuracy for population projections is weak at best, and forecasting beyond the short run involves considerable guesswork. A brief excursion into earlier Jewish population projections reveals that none has been an accurate prediction of the future, mainly because of the inability to predict disruptions or changes. Moreover, there is an uncanny similarity between the way projections were interpreted in the past and contemporary interpretations of future Jewish populations.

EARLY POPULATION PROJECTIONS AND THE JEWISH "PROBLEM"

Some of the first Jewish population projections were carried out in the late nineteenth and early twentieth centuries by social scientists con-

cerned about trends associated with the modernization and urbanization of societies and their impacts on Jewish communities. At that time,
demographic disparities between the Jewish communities in western
and eastern Europe were growing, because of the earlier modernization
of the former. The problematics of these increasing disparities, as
viewed by some, rested on the underlying assumption that the demographic and related patterns that were shaping the emergence of Jewish
communities in western Europe would, over time, also come to characterize the bulk of the Jewish population living in eastern Europe.

The major goal of these early Jewish population projections was to
demonstrate that the communities undergoing changes toward westernization and modernization were assimilating demographically (experiencing reduced fertility and smaller family size) through urbanization.
They were also believed to be losing their cohesive forms of Jewishness
through people's moving to places of fewer and weaker Jewish institutions. It was argued that some new form of Jewish population settlement (a "homeland") was needed to ensure a combination of dense Jewish
population, Jewish political control (i.e., the absence of minority status),
economic opportunity, and new forms of Jewish culture. In turn, the
new settlement would guarantee Jewish demographic survival and cultural renewal in the changing world of industrialization, nationalism,
and freedom. Population projections were designed to show that those
living in middle-class comfort in the west were facing the decline of
Judaism and Jewish culture (i.e., assimilating), whereas those in the east
were growing demographically at a rapid rate and suffering from
increasing poverty and economic discrimination. In short, population
projections were used to interpret the negative consequences of modernization among western European Jewish communities and the
impoverishment of Jews living in eastern Europe.[21]

Jewish population projections were designed to estimate or suggest
the implications of changes the communities were experiencing, particularly the decline in fertility and mortality in cities, the disruptive effects
of migration to urban areas, and the general trend toward assimilation.
These patterns were projected into the future to indicate the continued
decline of Jewishness in areas that were modernizing and the future
decline of the Jewish population everywhere. Many of these projections

were made by Zionists who used demographic tools to show the decline of Diaspora Jewish communities through fertility reduction and inter-marriage. Statisticians, many of whom were secular Jews, rejected the religious emphasis on residential density as a basis for communal cohesion and the negative reaction to modernity by the established leaders of Judaism as unacceptable to Jewish continuity in the Westernizing world. The interpretations of population projections were therefore consistent with the ideological positions emergent in late nineteenth- and early twentieth-century Europe: a general stance against minority group assimilation and a rejection of reforms in Judaism as alternatives to established Judaism.

Arthur Ruppin, the premier Jewish statistician and a Zionist,[22] used demographic data to show how urbanization and Westernization, migration to modern societies, and engagement in modern, industrially based occupations would result in the numerical decline of Jewish communities. Over time, he argued, these assimilatory tendencies would result in a weakening of the Jewish community. From his perspective, these tendencies, projected into the future, would require that Jews solve the "Jewish question" not by staying where they were (where they would face discrimination in eastern Europe) or by assimilating totally in western Europe. The solution to the problem of the social, economic, and political integration of Jews, and the only path to their modernization—along with the development of a secular Jewish culture—would be through immigration to Palestine. In a Jewish state, he argued, Jews would suffer none of the disabilities of minority status that they suffered in the Diaspora and would develop their own culture under Jewish political control. Demographic regeneration would occur along with the cultural and social renewal of the Jewish people. Rejecting the changes in Judaism and the continuing developments in Europe as solutions to the condition of Jews, he argued for secular Jewish culture and Jewish politics.

Ruppin and others used population projections to show the growth of the Jewish population in areas where Jews were poor—that is, in the small towns of eastern Europe, where marriages occurred at early ages and were almost universal—and the decline in Jewish population in western European countries, where fertility levels were low and intermarriage increasing. Under these assumptions, it took little imagination or technical skill to project the population into the future to show a decline of Jewish population in the west and an increase in poverty in the east. Erosion meant the decline of Jewish population numbers and the decrease of population quality. These patterns contradicted what many families were experiencing for the first time: the emergence of a middle class and high emigration rates from eastern Europe to the *goldena medena,* the golden country, the land of opportunity, the United States. For Ruppin as for others, this migration and social class mobility would only hasten the decline of Jewish populations. Demographic change would be rapid, fertility would decline with middle-class status, and Jewish culture would not develop outside the traditional Jewish communities of eastern Europe. The result, as Ruppin interpreted it, was that a viable solution to the Jewish "problem" was to change the course of these demographic patterns through a combination of nationalism, secularism, and emigration. The demographic data reinforced his preconceived notions of the contemporary demographic patterns and the inevitable future decline of Jewish communities based on them. Other demographers reached parallel conclusions about the demographic decline of western European Jews and the deteriorating quality of Jewish life in urban areas.

By the 1930s, when western and central Europe and the United States were in an economic and demographic depression, with low rates of growth in their general populations, the immigrant Jewish populations in the cities and in the middle classes were experiencing even lower rates of growth. Added to these general demographic patterns associated with the Jews were the growing but still low rates of Jewish intermarriage in Europe as political, social, and economic interactions between Jews and others increased. The "demographic problem" could be clearly documented by projecting into the future the implications of these contemporary patterns. By showing the consequences of the continuation of current demographic patterns, population projections demonstrated the urgent need to address the problem in more radical ways.

Few foresaw the emergence of American Jewish communities as a viable solution to these defined problems. American patterns, it was argued, were but an extension of the patterns of western Europe. Jews in the United States, too, would face threats of assimilation and discrimination, because the *goldena medena* was *trayfa* (unfit) for secular Zionists no less than for the Orthodox, although secular Zionists were a small minority of the total Jewish population in the United States. In fact, the longer-term growth of the American Jewish population through immigration and second-generation children does not appear to have been in jeopardy. Nor would these demographers consider that intermarriage might create a gain to the Jewish community through the incorporation of the non-Jewish-born partner. Intermarrying was defined as abandoning the Jewish community, rejecting one's origins, rather than as a basis for future Jewish population growth. This position was understandable, because rates of intermarriage were low and had little effect on Jewish population growth. Parents and their children viewed marriage outside the Jewish community as a sign of alienation and rejection. Rare events do not have to be incorporated into population projections.

POPULATION PROJECTIONS
FOR PALESTINE AND ISRAEL

If the first sets of Jewish population projections were associated with documenting the demographic "erosion" of Jews defined as living in the Diaspora, then forecasting Jewish population growth in Palestine was directed toward other conceptions of the future. Jewish population projections were regularly used in Palestine during the 1920s and 1930s to demonstrate the eventual size of the Jewish settlements there relative to the local Arab population and to the economic absorptive capacity of the country or the Jewish sector. These projections, prepared by the statisticians of the Jewish Agency (the Jewish governing body in Palestine under the British Mandate), particularly by Ruppin, were powerful demonstrations (at least for some period of time) of the need for increased Jewish immigration to Palestine.

Other projections, in the later 1930s and the 1940s, showed the Arab side. The increased Jewish presence in Palestine was significantly upsetting the ratio of Jews to Arabs, in favor of the Jewish population. The British and the Arabs interpreted this trend as a demographic threat to

Arabs' control over their own land. Population projections were published in various British white papers showing the need to regulate (control) Jewish immigration in order to continue the demographic dominance of the Arab population. The ongoing minority status of Jews in Palestine if immigration was regulated was the major basis for the justification, on the part of Arabs and the British, of more restrictive immigration policies and for the argument, on the part of Jews, for increased immigration. In the mid-1930s and subsequently, the British formulated a new demographic vision or policy for Palestine, one in which Arabs would remain the demographic majority, and Jews, a one-third minority.

The use of demographic projections to make political arguments about futures continued after the establishment of the State of Israel, particularly during the post-1967 period, when Israel's majority status was again challenged by its political action in controlling the West Bank and Gaza. A series of population projections was prepared in the early 1970s, when it was becoming clear that Israel was unlikely to immediately return the territories captured in the 1967 war. These projections were organized to spell out a range of scenarios and included estimates of fertility, mortality, and immigration for various Jewish and Arab populations.[23] Taking into account the higher Arab than Jewish fertility and Arabs' higher mortality, a series of population estimates was made to consider the relative proportions of Jews and Palestinians in the future. But here the question of the boundary of the territory and the populations to be included in the projections became critical. One of the most intriguing interpretations of these multiple projections was that the retention of all the territories captured by Israel in 1967, along with their Arab populations, would make Jews a minority in about two generations, whatever the level of Jewish immigration.

One of the conclusions was that if the territories were incorporated into Israel, then the state's Jewishness would be threatened even as its democratic character was retained. This conclusion was ironic, because it was the more nationalistic (and religious) political parties in Israel that had advocated incorporating the territories and their Arab population. The alternative conclusion, that a colonial-type state would result from retaining the territories but not incorporating their Arab populations as citizens of Israel, came closer to the reality. These demographic projections were designed not to predict the future but to suggest the future consequences of past trends so that they might be prevented. Given the implications of the projections, the message was clear: change the policy regarding the administered territories or in the future Israel will have a demographic configuration and a social composition that is undesirable for Jews. Others (the more nationalistic territorialists) argued for increased Jewish immigration to Israel, in order to out-populate the Arabs and retain a Jewish demographic majority and Jewish control. But despite its value to the state, increased immigration was always difficult to manage from Israel, except in cases of Jewish populations in political distress.

CONCLUSION

The major point to reiterate about Jewish population projections is that they are unlikely to be useful as predictions or forecasts of the future. Their value is extremely limited; they reflect more an assessment of contemporary conditions and conceptions of the future than predictions of actual future populations. Hence, and more importantly, policy makers should be extremely reluctant to use population forecasts for their goals of enhancing Jewish continuity. Demographic experts and non-experts alike should exercise extreme caution in interpreting the results of such demographic exercises. The social science view of population projections is that they will be used to reinforce preconceived notions of social change and ideological commitments. In that sense, population projections should be studied as reflections of the biases of those who interpret them, and not as bases for innovative or creative policies.

One overriding conclusion from this brief excursion into the world of population projections is that the Jewish future is not threatened by its demography. The fundamental question for studying the Jewish future is the quality of Jewish life, not the quantity of Jewish population. It is to questions of how we know the content of Jewish quality and how it can be measured that I now turn.

4

THE CENTRALITY OF JEWISH VALUES

IN SHAPING THE JEWISH FUTURE

The issue of the Jewish future is not primarily quantitative. I have argued from the quantitative evidence and from the limitations of population projections that the futures of Jewish communities must be assessed in terms of the quality of Jewish life. My questions are, What kinds of Jewish communities are likely to emerge in the twenty-first century? What will characterize their Jewishness and their Judaism? What will Jewish culture look like in the future? Will it connect to the historical values of the past? Will Jewish values be distinctive in comparison with the values of others who are likely to be similar to Jews socially, economically, and politically?

To address these qualitative questions we need to uncover ways to identify the sources and contexts of Jewish quality in life. These are grand themes, and few social science guidelines are available that are useful for the task. Most observers have avoided specifying the quality of Jewish life, largely because definitions of it directly address core arenas of disagreement and conflict within the community. There are no simple, agreed-upon indicators of Jewish quality among Jewish leaders. One group's Jewish quality is unlikely to be shared by others. The Orthodox, for example, might define Jewish quality along lines of ritual observance, whereas Jewish secular organizations might focus on philanthropy. Reform rabbis might define Jewish quality in terms of ethical and moral values, whereas Zionist organizations might focus on commitment to the State of Israel. These are cogent elements of Jewish values, and together they reflect the complexities of Jewish culture. Yet few anchors of Jewish values are shared by everyone defined as Jews.

In this and the following chapter, I develop three themes based on different methodological strategies. These are somewhat unusual for a sociologist, so they require some justification. The first strategy, which I employ in this chapter, is that of oral history; the next chapter reviews rabbinic conceptions of prophesy and analyzes biblical conceptions of animal sacrifices that help me articulate a Jewish conception of values and of Jewish futures.

The methodological basis of this chapter is that one way to examine Jewish values is through life histories. I recognize that ethnographies have a variety of substantive uses. I have never before used ethnographic research, except to demonstrate its methodological weaknesses. However, my students in anthropological demography and some of my colleagues have regularly argued for its value. I am slowly being convinced that mixed methodological strategies, combining quantitative and qualitative research, maximize the value of one's analysis. So I turn to ethnography to illustrate changes in Jewish values over the life course and to explore changing images of Jewish futures.

I use the following partial biography of an Israeli man named Shmuel Braw to explore how different sources of information might be used to interpret the ways in which social scientists understand futures in specific contexts. The social and family contexts that people experience shape the conceptions they have of futures, and social scientists are no exception. Their conceptions of the Jewish future are shaped by the values and contexts of their lives, just as population projections are influenced by the contexts in which they are organized.

SHMUEL'S FUTURE

He was a typical extraordinary Jew. His name was Shmuel Braw.[1] He regularly sat next to me at the synagogue in Talpiot, Jerusalem. From time to time during the various learned talks, at other intervals during the prayers, and on the walk home on Friday evenings, he told me tantalizing stories about his life, half in Yiddish and half in Australian-accented English with a strong Polish twist.

He went to bed quite late, he said, so that he'd be certain of sleeping till the next morning. Sometimes the nightmares woke him, and then he knew he wouldn't go to sleep again. He did not describe his nightmares. Knowing that he had lost his wife, their only daughter, his mother, two sisters, their husbands and children, and countless other relatives and friends during the Second World War, and learning that he himself was a survivor of a Siberian labor camp, it was not hard to imagine what he dreamed about.

I began to interview Shmuel in order to put a human face on the larger picture of European Jewish transformation that I was studying.[2] I wanted to know whether I could illustrate the themes of change among Jewish communities with qualitative insights from diverse persons of European origins living in Jerusalem. I failed to carry out that part of the project, but I had another motive in this exploration—the need to learn about the sources of Jewish values. And I discovered that Shmuel had many things to teach other people about Jewish values and about how we should think about Jewish futures.

Tarnow

Shmuel was born around the turn of the twentieth century in Tarnow, a middle-size city about forty-five miles east of Cracow, in the Galicia sector of Poland. Initially I was curious about why he and millions of others like him had chosen to remain in Poland rather than follow the large stream of emigration to the United States, the land of opportunity, where "the streets were paved with gold." Had they emigrated to America, they would have been spared the horrors of the Second World War. The answer he gave was straightforward. He and his family had remained in Tarnow largely because they were doing well economically, with good prospects for continuing to live in prosperity. His clients in the lumber and coal business were local, his family and economic networks were powerful, and his family was economically comfortable in Poland. Tarnow was home to him. His friends were there, his languages were Polish and Yiddish, and his family was important to him. There appeared to be no reason for him to live elsewhere. His view of the future at that point in his life was positive. Indeed, his description of life in Poland in the 1920s and 1930s parallels in many ways the stories one reads about life among American Jews of Polish origins living in New York and other places where poor Jewish immigrants from eastern Europe settled and became American. For him and many of his friends, Tarnow was home. Life was good, and the future seemed bright.

To be sure, anti-Semitism and discrimination existed, and Tarnow's Jews did not have all the rights and privileges that non-Jews had in Poland. But these attitudes and limitations were not new in the 1920s and 1930s. Social mobility and assimilation were the hallmarks of the day, and the Jews of Tarnow experienced improvements in their lifestyle. Theater, art and travel, lectures, and schmoozing with the boys were the pastimes of middle-class Jewish men in Poland, just as in the United States. Shmuel described these activities with great enthusiasm, not only to mark what he had lost but also to convey the richness of his past life. His future appeared to him to be rosy, full of excitement and possibilities. He was an optimist. Life was improving for him and his family. Even in retrospect he spoke of the beautiful life in Tarnow before the Second World War.

What did the future look like to Shmuel Braw in the late 1930s in Poland? He was married, a father, and a prosperous businessman, self-confident and increasingly active in the Jewish community. He expected his Jewish community and his lifestyle to continue for the rest of his and his family's lives. Certainly he had no reason to expect that a holocaust was coming from Germany that would engulf Tarnow and destroy almost every vestige of Jewish life there—the institutions, the Jewish buildings, and all the people who lived in them. Despite the challenges of survival some Jews faced due to poverty, discrimination, and other hardships, Shmuel expected that the Jews of Tarnow would continue to live there for centuries, as they had for centuries past. Most members of the Jewish community of Tarnow probably thought that it had a future, and that their own future was bound up with Tarnow's.

Touching evidence of the culture of the Jews of Tarnow can be found in a memorial volume published in Yiddish by the Association of Tarnow Jews after the war. It is a work of well over eight hundred pages, containing a long survey of the five-hundred-year history of the Jews in Tarnow and many shorter articles about different aspects of Jewish life there. This volume is one of scores like it, all published after the Holocaust by survivors, commemorating their towns. Simply to go to a library and read the names on the spines of these books is an over-whelming experience, as if the lives, energies, and concerns of millions of people have been compressed between the covers and arranged in alphabetical order on shelves. One feels that those lives might spill out of the volumes if one picked them up and opened them. These books reveal a different view of the living communities of Europe from that implied by the millions of names of Holocaust victims memorialized at Yad Vashem in Jerusalem.

One lesson about the future emerges clearly—many people, both Jews and non-Jews, stay where they are and expect to remain where they are when they have family roots, networks, and opportunities. Even when circumstances become very difficult, many people feel no wanderlust.

Tarnow was a heterogeneous city where religious and secular Jews lived, where Zionists and socialists argued, and where most of the Jewish community took care of its own. Shmuel was a capitalist businessman, but he supported socialist groups because the socialists were "doing things for the community." Shmuel reported to me: "I gave money to the Zionists, but I wouldn't vote for them, because the only party that was doing something for the Jews in Tarnow was the socialists." The Zionists "were doing a good job," he added, "but they weren't interested in local life. They only cared about the future. A thousand years from now, a dream. The real situation didn't interest them. Socialists were trying to help the people."

Shmuel's early adult life recedes into the background of his story as the war and the Holocaust emerge in the late 1930s and 1940s. Shmuel last saw his daughter alive on a truck with her schoolmates, being taken by Nazis to the outskirts of Tarnow. The Nazis never had a chance to shoot them, because their teachers gave them poison chocolates on the truck in order to avoid the crueler death awaiting them. Shmuel and other Jews buried their children on the edge of the city.

Shmuel survived the war, though barely, through ingenuity and luck. Surviving the Holocaust appeared to be a random fate in those cities and towns where most were killed.

Returning Home

After World War II, Shmuel returned to Tarnow, as he had with his family after World War I, in the hope that he might reconnect with his wife. She had been transported, so he thought, to the labor camp at Auschwitz—"labor camp" being a term not yet known to him as a synonym for genocide. He returned to Tarnow but was unprepared for what he found. He described what he witnessed as follows:

"Nothing, a cemetery."

Shmuel's voice sounds as if his mouth is still full of gall.

"The whole city was a cemetery. I mean the Jewish part. Nothing. Doesn't exist." Now he is angry. "From the buildings is left only roofs, no windows, no doors. Rubbish. Rubble. Everywhere the streets are full of that. Nothing. Nothing."

When one thinks of the Holocaust, one thinks mainly of the murders, an inconceivable number of individual murders. One forgets the destruction of property, of monuments and community buildings, of houses, synagogues, schools, clubs, hospitals, and shops. These were the material creations of tightly knit communities that had thrived in one spot for generations. Shmuel was a man with a highly developed sense of place. And his place was utterly destroyed. Even before reliable information about the extent of the tragedy was available, the physical annihilation of the Jewish half of the town meant that everything—that is, the community—was gone.

Shmuel stayed in Tarnow for a few months, housed by the Jewish welfare organization in some buildings on the outskirts of the ghetto, living in Jewish property recovered after the war. "Maybe the owners were dead," Shmuel speculated.

"How did you feel?" I asked.

"You are not lonely," he tells me. His voice is strangled; the words are almost swallowed. "You are not lonely but lost. You follow me?"

Then he gives me a clinical description of apathy. "People without life. You want nothing. You just want death." His voice strains. "Without feeling anything. And that with everybody the same."

Then one feeling emerged: the overwhelming need to leave Tarnow and Poland as soon as possible.

Were you shocked when you first returned to Tarnow?" I asked.

"Shocked?" he asks indulgently, with a smile he reserved for a particularly silly question. "What do you mean, shocked? I couldn't sleep for weeks at a time. I was wandering around. I couldn't sleep. You know I was in that street where I lived with my first wife and child about a dozen times."

His voice lowers almost to a whisper. "And up to the house where I was living. I couldn't go in."

It was a rented apartment in a neighborhood that was not walled in when the Nazis created the Jewish ghetto. Many of Shmuel's belongings were probably still there. But he couldn't force himself over the threshold.

His parents' house was nearby. He walked by it more than a dozen times, but again he couldn't go in. He did enter his oldest sister's house, a new one. A Polish family now occupied it. Shmuel went in to talk to the new "lady of the house" and was surprised to see his sister's furniture, unharmed and in the same places. He says that on the way back to his rented room some five kilometers away, "excuse me, I was vomiting all the way back. I was meshugge. I was sure I was finished. I was sick a week's time in bed."

Shmuel has some pictures taken in Tarnow in 1946. One shows a broken column with Hebrew letters carved on it. The survivors had erected a memorial in the Jewish cemetery, where Shmuel said Jews were buried in eight mass graves. The picture of the memorial doesn't affect me much: a broken pillar from the synagogue with a simple inscription. I have seen too many memorials. I am more shaken when I hear that every Jewish survivor in Tarnow placed a stone in the commemorative wall visible behind the pillar, listing the names of his or her family members who perished. "On my stone there were seventeen names," Shmuel tells me. That is a statistic one can grasp.

An extended family was reduced to a handful of isolated survivors. What is left of Shmuel's Tarnow? The Jewish houses and institutions no longer stand. Nine-tenths of the Jews who lived there were murdered. Those who survived now live in a dozen cities on every continent in the world. The close-knit community that shaped Shmuel's personality and fostered his development had been ripped to shreds. Shmuel was one of its tattered remnants, and he still yearned for the whole cloth from which he was torn.

He never lost his vitality, however. He shows me another photograph. It is of himself, neat, clean, and well dressed. Next to him, smiling shyly, is an attractive young woman, Esther, his second wife.

Esther had appeared in Uzbekistan toward the end of the war with a small group of young Ukrainian Jews, following up rumors of the survival of her relatives. Her village in Ukraine had been completely destroyed. When repatriation began, she and some other people with nowhere else to go joined up with Shmuel in search of a new life. They thought they might find it in Tarnow.

Once there, however, they quickly recognized that their only hope for living a normal life was to leave again. "I will do everything I can to get out," said Shmuel, remembering his thinking in 1946. "You can't live in a cemetery."

Shmuel told me that he and other survivors of Tarnow "saw that they had to come back to a normal life. You know what I mean? You fell in the mud. But you can't stay dirty all your life. True or not?" Then he quotes a popular Yiddish poem, *Die Goldene Kait*, "The Golden Chain." You have to keep adding links to the golden chain. That was the theme of our discussions at night. He and his fellow survivors weren't prepared to give up.

I asked, "What made you want to live after what you had seen?" He takes my provocatively blunt question seriously. It is legitimate to wonder about such things, he tells me. Half coyly and half arrogantly, Shmuel reverts to his self-definition as a rebel and denies that he found a religious answer. For years he couldn't find God, but he rediscovered the power of Jewish history and the value of Jewish community. He said, "First thing, you've got a feeling that they won't destroy the Jewish people. We wanted to build up a Jewish life to what it was in Poland. But that was impossible."

He and Esther made their way, with thousands of others, across the Czech border, then into Austria, and finally to Italy, where the refugees awaited individual solutions to their problems. New destinations were sought to put an end to their displacement.

Esther and Shmuel had made their way in trucks and by foot from

Poland to Italy, on their way to Palestine. Hundreds, thousands of Polish Jews walking to Italy. Surely an amazing sight.

Melbourne

But Shmuel was not to arrive in Palestine so soon. There was too much conflict there at the time. His brother, who had moved to Palestine in the 1920s as part of the young socialist-Zionist pioneer movement, dissuaded him from coming. It was too difficult, he wrote to Shmuel. So he selected a place as far away from his Tarnow as he could find. He ended up in Melbourne, Australia, for twenty-five years.

The Jewish community in Melbourne sponsored a number of refugees. Shmuel left Italy when he was forty-three, with an infant daughter and his pregnant wife, Esther, knowing several languages but not a word of English.

I asked him if he had been optimistic about the future at this point in his life. Had he felt that he would be able to recapture in Melbourne the Jewish way of life he had lived in Tarnow? Melbourne had thousands of Jews, a rich set of Jewish institutions, synagogues, and stores, and thousands of refugees from the European Holocaust. How was Melbourne different from Tarnow? I asked.

"In Melbourne life was normal, but not in a Jewish way."

As much as I pressed and probed, I could learn little about Shmuel's life in Melbourne. It simply wasn't his community. I wanted to learn about other Jewish communities in Australia, how he related to the beauty and scenery, to the Aborigines, and to the long-term residents, how he might have enjoyed the Great Barrier Reef or the vastness of the outback, the theater, the opera, the arts. But these were not Shmuel's experiences in Australia. As a young man he had been a great European traveler, and he described in rich detail such features of Poland. But somehow his experiences in Tarnow before and after the war led him not to explore Australia. He never left Melbourne, never visited other places in the country. Never traveled or toured.

He and Esther survived in Melbourne, raised their two daughters, and worked hard. But Melbourne was never home.

Jerusalem

After moving to Jerusalem to retire and joining one of his daughters who was living there, Shmuel forgot about Melbourne, he said. He even forgot the names of the streets he had lived on. But he never forgot Tarnow. He was now a Jerusalemite, he told me with some pride and a little unease.

When pressed, he would not call himself a Zionist, although he did concede that in his view the future of most Jewish communities in the world was bound up with the future of Israel. He remembered his feelings after World War II. While he and Esther were in transit in Italy, he said, "We looked around. We could see that the Jews were a different kind of people. Not in looks. How they are dressed. In behavior. Just going around like a *hind in a dorf* [a stray dog]. Afraid of something. Always afraid of something. You see two Italians, you know it's their land. We are strangers." Unlike in Italy or Melbourne, Shmuel was not a stranger in Tarnow or Jerusalem.

When Shmuel was first married, he was a vigorous man in his midtwenties, well known in his hometown and employed in a prospering family business. His future seemed to offer him steady progress toward wealth, comfort, and influence—an enviable prospect. Sixteen years later, as he entered into a second marriage, what could he reasonably expect? There was no way of knowing. He did not know where he would settle, what new language he would have to learn, or how he could support himself. In Poland at this age he would have had the prospect of easing off and passing some of the burden on to a nephew or son-in-law. After the war, it was clear that there would be no continuity for him in Poland.

Sometimes Shmuel felt depressed: he could see no future for Judaism. The war had uprooted the plant and poisoned its native soil. I asked, "So where am I supposed to get my *yiddishkeit,* my Jewishness? If Tarnow and places like Tarnow contained the only authentic Judaism, and they are all destroyed, then what about the people born after the destruction? Where can they find 'authentic' Jewishness?" Shmuel was hard hit by the question. "I don't have an answer," he said. From his point of view, current Judaism was without foundations.

I asked the question in a different way: "How can your daughter Rivka manage to live a full Jewish life? Where does she draw her Jewishness?"

"She agrees with me," Shmuel answered. "She got it from her parents."

"So won't her children get it from her?" I asked.

Shmuel was not sure. Living in Israel was not enough. He saw Judaism getting weaker and weaker as time went on.

But I refused to let up. I remembered Shmuel's telling me that his three-year-old grandson already knew the Modeh Ani, the first morning prayer—"I thank You, O living and eternal King, for returning my soul to me in mercy. Great is Your faithfulness."

"Don't you feel wonderful when you hear your grandson say the Modeh Ani, Shmuel?" I asked almost rhetorically.

"Yes," he admitted, "I do."

Shmuel is buried in the cemetery of the kibbutz where his daughter and her family have made a home for themselves. He spent the last few years of his life there, uprooted again from Jerusalem by rising housing costs and failing health, lost and unconnected beyond his family. The last time I saw him, he had lost much of his energy and most of his memory. But his stories and his dreams about the future live on in the children and grandchildren he loved, and in the lives of others whom he touched and to whom he revealed these stories.

THOUGHTS ON SHMUEL'S FUTURE

Shmuel's is one of thousands of stories that have been recorded about the lives of people who lived through some of the major upheavals of the last century and the major events of Jewish history. His story is unique but also illustrative. His experiences in their specific contexts are particular to him. Yet I suggest that important insights into the nature of Jewish communities and the values that cement the lives of Jews can be gleaned from carefully reconstructed and analyzed oral histories. We can learn much about Jewish values and futures from Shmuel's reconstruction of his past.

Shmuel held several different conceptions of the future throughout his life. In each case his conception was based on his contemporary circumstances. When he returned to Tarnow after the First World War, his conception of his future and that of his extended family in Tarnow was positive. In contrast, when he returned after the Second World War, he rejected Poland as a place for his future life. His earlier optimism and later pessimism about the future reflected the radically different contexts of his life and his community at the two times. But he never gave up on some kind of future for himself and his new family.

While he was in Italy, his conception of his future included Palestine, but he rejected that option for himself at the time. He had rejected God as part of his future when he felt abandoned, and he foresaw little future for Judaism. His future was infused with family and community, even though it was no longer clear to him where he would find a community. He had been a religious Jew, observant of weekly and seasonal rituals and attending the synagogue daily. Now, he said, he had lost his belief, and he would deny that he was as religious as his pious parents and grandparents. He spoke Yiddish to his friends and family and sang beautiful Jewish tunes. His Jewishness was the *yiddishkeit* part of his soul, which he could not reject even if he wanted to. While he was in Australia, he developed a commitment to his future and that of his family, first in Melbourne and then in Israel. He left one daughter, a successful attorney in Melbourne, to join his other daughter in Jerusalem. He was divided by his family's choices.

During his last days, living in Israel, his future was connected to the lives of his grandchildren on a religious kibbutz. Melbourne and Australia were different places from Tarnow and Poland; Jerusalem and Israel were different still from his prior places of residence. But despite these radical changes of location in his life, Shmuel knew that there were forms of Jewish cultural continuity. He expressed enormous pride in his grandson's recitation of the morning prayer that he himself had recited in various countries and that, most likely, his ancestors had recited when they were children.

Researchers use oral histories to shed light on the past and for understanding the present. What is the role of oral history in studying the Jewish future? At first glance the answer is that oral history is the least likely methodological strategy for understanding how people perceive the future. But on closer inspection, oral history may be an underutilized strategy for understanding how conceptions of the future shape actions in the present and underpin decision making. People decide among alternatives as they consider future possibilities and options for themselves and their children. More importantly, it may be one strategy for understanding the role of values in shaping people's lives. Values are always anchored in contexts. Structure provides possibilities; values help mold the ways in which we take advantage of these possibilities and opportunities. Shmuel Braw's story is the story not simply of one survivor but of many persons in the Jewish community.

Even within the lifetime of one person we can reconstruct the various meanings of futures and learn important rules for disentangling the processes of social change at the individual level and at the level where individuals and their communities interact. The Modeh Ani, for example, was something culturally and Jewishly familiar that Shmuel had said to his grandfather and that his grandson recited to him.

Because conceptions of the future are conditioned by the contexts of the present, futures that we perceive are always best conceptualized not as predictions but as values. Jews transmit values in ways that might never have been seen before, but these values are real as Jewishness is strengthened in new ways. The kibbutz that Shmuel experienced in his last days was not Tarnow, and his relationship with his grandchildren in Israel was something he could never have imagined in the early post–World War II years.

In the end, Shmuel saw his role in shaping the future as one of helping to transmit a core of Jewish values to his children and grandchildren. That core was a familiar prayer recited by rote. The prayer resonated not from the meaning of its content but from Shmuel's experiences and his grandson's recitation. That great golden chain of generational continuity in families, the transmission of cultural items, whatever they may be, represents one of the core Jewish values—values that are transformed in new contexts through new experiences.

Oral histories, rich in individual perceptions of families and communities, are the living books from which we can learn about the deepest Jewish values and how they have been and can be transmitted generationally. They reveal stories about values in contexts. They do not reveal much about communities or institutions. For that we must turn elsewhere and use different strategies of discovery.

What are the other sources of Jewish values that go beyond the personal, the familial, and the idiosyncratic? How might we get a peek at some core Jewish values that transcend generations and are reinterpreted in history? I now turn briefly to Jewish sacred texts for some insights into how contemporary Jewish values can be discerned in traditional textual materials.

5

WHAT PROPHECY AND ANIMAL

SACRIFICES REVEAL ABOUT

CONTEMPORARY JEWISH COMMUNITIES

To explore the sources of the values that make contemporary Jewish communities distinctive, I turn to two sets of texts that have been defined as sacred by Jews. These texts, all from the Hebrew Bible, deal with the themes of prophecy and animal sacrifices. Excursions into biblical texts and analyses of the role of prophets are not the usual disciplinary interests of social scientists focusing on contemporary societies. My goal is not to systematically review the biblical literature on animal sacrifices and prophecy or the meanings these things had at the time the texts were written or in the minds of later generations. Instead, my objective is to use an authentic Jewish source for understanding some of the key values that are emergent in contemporary Jewish communities. The analysis is not meant to convey that these particular passages from the Hebrew Bible are the only or the major or the best sources for these values, or that the text primarily means what I have inferred from it. Rather, I use these texts as sources for some of the fundamental ideas I have about Jewish values.

PROPHECY AND FUTURES

In addition to learning values from social experiences, from family members and peers, and from stories conveyed generationally, people learn values from interpretations of texts. Some ancient texts reinforce the cultural core of a religion and are reinterpreted regularly to address new generations. In Jewish life, certain books have been defined as holy or sacred and are selectively taught to children and adults. They are often read at religious services, used by rabbis in their sermons, and discussed on holidays and at religious events. Many contain stories holding the kernels of values that have been interpreted differently by those who are defined as the legitimate Jewish cultural interpreters. They have also been interpreted differently over the generations. From these interpretations we may be able to learn about values and conceptions of the future.

Let me illustrate by examining the sourcebook of Jewish values—the Tanach, or the Hebrew Bible—and its conception of the future. The personification of the futurist in the Tanach is the *navi*, the prophet, whose role is one of several social roles outlined in the Tanach. Prophets are often models of holiness and represent the values underlying conceptions of the future.

The prophet is often depicted as God's mouthpiece, someone who has access to the divine council and its deliberations. That is often where prophets receive their oracles. Some prophets are ecstatics—they see visions. Certain aspects of their behavior are routinized and predictable. They may be viewed in part as social and political commentators. Some work for the government; others are peripheral critics. The prophet's role as a futurist is but one of many roles the text specifies for him or her. When and how the futurist role of prophets is emphasized therefore becomes the analytic question.

The Torah, the first five books of the Tanach, defines some of the various administrative roles for the emerging community of Jewish people. Judges, administrative officials, priests, Levites, and kings all have specified roles. So do prophets.

In the fifth book of the Torah, Deuteronomy, chapters 16–18, the roles of various political and administrative leaders are described. The text teaches us the following about the prophet (Deut. 18:15): "The Lord your God will raise up for you a prophet from among your own people, like myself [Moses]; him shall you heed." The *navi*, then, is to be selected from among the Jewish people, eliminating non-Jews and foreigners.[1] More importantly, the *navi* is not isolated from the community but a part of it. The prophet is an observer of the community but is distinctive within it. "From among your own people" suggests both locus, or place, and class of person.

The text continues: "God said to me [Moses] . . . I will raise up a prophet for them from among their own people like yourself; I will put My words in his mouth and he will speak to them all that I command him. And if anybody fails to heed the words he speaks in My name, I Myself will call him to account" (Deut. 18:17–19).

Here, God tells the *navi* what to report. There is no indication that the *navi* takes any personal initiative; he seems to be the conduit for God's words. At least, this is one core conception in the Torah, if not one necessarily shared by all of the prophets. The prophet reports God's word. The *navi* conveys words in his or her own idiom and style, but the ideas are God's. The content of the prophet's message is God's; the form is the *navi*'s.

How can we tell whether the words of the prophet are the message of God? The Torah presents two tests of the prophet's truthfulness. First, "a prophet who presumes to speak in God's name an oracle that I did not command him to utter, or who speaks in the name of other gods— that prophet shall die" (Deut. 18:20). That is, if the prophet conveys a content that suggests a false god, he is liable for punishment. So content is one of the elements of truthfulness among prophets.

More directly, Deuteronomy 18 ends with a fascinating and puzzling two verses that specify the second element of prophecy and address the question of how one can differentiate between true and false prophecies: "And should you ask yourselves, 'How can we know that the oracle was not spoken by the Lord?' If the prophet speaks in the name of the Lord and the oracle does not come true, the oracle was not spoken by the Lord; the prophet has uttered it presumptuously. You should not fear him" (Deut. 18:21–22).

According to the text, the *navi* conveys the word of God and at times predicts future events. If the *navi*'s predictions do not come about, then she or he has spoken falsely. The decision about whether the navi has spoken God's word is left to the judgment of people of the future. The judgment is not to be made by way of miracles and not by some additional revelation. Rather, people decide on the basis of whether or not the prediction came to pass. The people are the arbiters of the future,

not on the basis of the prophet's popularity but on the basis of empirical evidence. The need for a *navi* as the conveyor of God's word in no
way absolves people of their responsibility to decide, at least in retrospect, whether the *navi's* predictions of the future were true. This is a
very rigid test. The wise prophet either steers away from predictions or
makes them vague and well into the future. Hence, the *navi's* predictions are not useful in the present when people need to make policy decisions or decide how to behave religiously or ritually.

Thus, the contents of prophecies and their accuracy are the elements
that determine their truthfulness. It is not the prophet who foretells the
future, but God. The people are to judge in retrospect whether the prophet
gave voice to God's message accurately. The problem, of course, is that
we often need to make judgments today about the truth of a prediction
and act accordingly. We cannot wait for the future to inform us about
the truth of the past. Therefore, in the two tests of the prophet's truthfulness, content is always more powerful (more immediate) than accurate prediction of the future.

A brief examination of the prophets of the Torah reveals much about
their role. The first designated prophet is Abraham (Gen. 20:7). He is
defined as a *navi* whose role is to intercede on behalf of others. He is a
prophet because God engages in a dialogue with him. He is a spokesper-
son who receives the call from God. This is the critical element in defining
prophecy, although it is not a test of the content of his prophecy. Moses
is referred to as a special prophet: "Never again did there arise in Israel
a prophet like Moses" (Deut. 34:10). But that was only one of his roles,
since Moses was primarily a lawgiver and not a predictor of the future.

The Talmud notes that the prophets neither took away nor added to
the Torah (except for the reading of the Megillah—Talmud Bavli,
Megillah, 14A). Moses and the rest of the prophets did not add to the
words of God. They conveyed them.

What about prophets in the post-Tanach period? Do we have prophets
in contemporary times?[2] In part the answer depends on whether we stick
to the biblical definition of prophecy—speaking divine words, envisioning
what others cannot see, critiquing society.

The rabbis of the Talmud obviously were committed to studying the
messages of God as conveyed by the prophets and included study of the

prophets as part of the worship service. But they had some ambivalence about prophets. Note that in the opening part of *Pirkay Avot,* Ethics of the Fathers, prophets are listed as the conveyors of the Torah in a chain extending from Moses, but they otherwise have no specialized or over-riding role. The first paragraph of the first chapter of *Avot* states that Moses *received* the Torah on Sinai (*kebale,* "received," as opposed to *mes-sarah,* "transmitted") and conveyed it to Joshua, who transmitted it to the elders. They transmitted it to the prophets, who in turn transmitted it to the rabbis of the Great Assembly. There is no special role for the prophets in the great chain of tradition except as transmitters of the law and its values.

Further, the Talmud teaches that after the deaths of the last of the prophets (Hagai, Zechariah, and Malachi), the holy spirit of prophetic inspiration departed from Israel, and the Jews were able to avail them-selves only of the *bat kol*—the divine voice, secondary to prophecy (Talmud Bavli, Sanhedrin, 11A).

Who gets to be defined as a prophet in the post-prophetic period? Naturally, there is a Talmudic disagreement (Talmud Bavli, Baba Batra, 12AB): "Rav Adimi from Haifa said: 'Since the days when the Temple was destroyed, prophecy has been taken from the prophets and given to the wise.' [So God reveals himself to the *chachamim,* the sages, at least in the view of those sages who wrote the Talmud]. Rabbi Yohanan said: 'Since the Temple was destroyed, prophecy was taken from prophets and given to fools and children' [only false prophets remain]."

Why were the rabbis of the Talmud so concerned about the end of prophecy? Every Jewish religious philosopher from Maimonides in the twelfth century to Heschel in the twentieth considered prophecy and the message of the prophets to be the source of some of the core values of Judaism. For Maimonides, the highest form of prophecy was the for-mulation of divine law, whereas in lower forms prophecy entailed instruction in adherence to the law. Heschel argued that the prophet not only was the conduit of God but also was in dialogue with God. Others, such as Soloveitchik, argued that the prophet's dialogue with God made possible the establishment of the covenant between God and the Jewish people as God's community. Ahad Ha'am, Asher Ginsberg, the so-called agnostic rabbi, ruled out the supernatural element of prophecy and viewed the prophet as the manifestation of the Jewish national spirit. Thus, each of the philosophers viewed the role of the prophet within his own scheme, fitting the prophet into a broader theoretical framework.

The answer to the question about why the Talmudic rabbis rejected the active role of contemporary prophets is partly that they feared a distortion of the role of the prophet and were reacting to false prophets who preached new additions to and subtractions from the Torah. Moreover, several of the more illustrious biblical prophets, such as Jonah and Micah, preached futures that did not come about. The rejection of contemporary prophecy was primarily in negative reaction to Christianity, which, in the view of the rabbis, emerged with a "prophet" who advocated changes in the Torah as a basis for a "new" testament.

But there is a more fundamental reason for their rejection of the role of the prophet as a futurist. And this reason goes to the heart of Judaism as an emergent religious system. The rabbinical or normative Judaism of the Talmud is a Judaism based on ethics and morals, as well as on the law (Halacha) and its development. The promulgation of the law is not the primary role of the prophet. Some prophets, such as Amos, enforced legal norms; others critiqued kings and the powerful from the vantage point of Israelite legal traditions. Legal expertise is not the expertise of the *navi*. It would be a chaotic system indeed if people claimed to hear the word of God, promulgated new laws and eliminated old ones, and the community then had to wait for some sign in the future in order to determine whether these visions had been correct. A religion based on law is unusual and demanding. It is not simply a religion of belief, of being Jewish, but a religion of action, of *doing* Jewishness. If one had to wait until prophecy was deemed true in the future, one would be unable to act at all.[3]

Judaisms are based on the Torah and on the development of rabbinic law and interpretation, not on prophecies of the future. Of course the rabbis of the Talmud had to be supportive of the value of the ancient prophets and to incorporate the words and ideas of the prophets, who were the conduits of God's message. In turn, they had to apply those principles to situations that the prophets did not experience, using an idiom that the prophets did not use. Each prophet speaks in his or her idiom, the idiom of his or her world, even as all true prophets speak the word of God without innovation, addition, or subtraction. It is others, not the prophets, who have to develop the law, the Halacha, in the context of the principles and messages of the prophets. The legal experts are the innovators. Prophets are primarily messengers.

The rabbis encouraged Jews to remember Moses as Moshe *rabbenu,* "Moses our teacher," not as Moses the *navi,* the prophet. It is "Abraham our forefather" *(Avenu),* not Abraham the prophet, who sets the course for future generations. It is the rabbis and teachers, the religious functionaries who carry on the traditions of teaching the Torah and interpreting Jews' obligations and responsibilities in innovative ways, who substitute for the role of prophet. They are not passive but active, not God's conduits but initiators and interpreters. The role of the prophet has become more specialized and "limited" to interpreting the present, not predicting the future. It was the role undertaken by the rabbis, the teachers, that transformed the futurism of the prophet into the conduit of the legitimate religious message. Indeed, all Jews, not only the religious functionaries, have inherited the transformed role of prophet. It is their responsibility to shape the future and see to it that Jewish ideals are worked out as the true word of God and his prophets.

Prophecy as an examination of the future is of limited value in Judaism. Prophets convey the messages, but the people decide whether the messages are true and accurate. Their interpretations of the future, like their interpretations of prophecy, are best understood as part of the broader context of their values. Jews' orientation to the future and its possibilities reflect not predictions of the future but understandings of the past and the present. Indeed, how Jews understand the past may reflect how they imagine the future, just as their understanding of the future is anchored in their conceptions of the past. The value of the prophet as futurist is determined by the accuracy of the prediction. The role of the prophet is of value in terms of the content of the messages that are conveyed. When content is the central theme, we need to turn to other roles to learn new content and innovative messages.

ANIMAL SACRIFICES AND VALUES

The sacred texts of the ancient Israelites outlined other roles besides that of prophet. Among the most important were the roles of priests *(kohanim)* and Levites. They were primarily in charge of the sacrificial system and the temple, although they were medical diagnosticians and healers as well. They had an instructional manual: the rabbis of the Talmud referred to most of the third book of the Hebrew Bible, Leviticus, as *Torat Kohanim,* the Law or Handbook for Priests.

The book of Leviticus focuses on animal and other sacrifices—their types, regulations, and procedures. It prescribes in meticulous detail what is to be burned and what is to be consumed, by whom, and how. On the surface, it appears particularly uninteresting for most Jews living in twenty-first-century America, Europe, or Israel. The specific content of Leviticus seems to be irrelevant, removed from modern Jewish society and modern lives. At best, Jews today believe its themes were an appropriate guide during the temple period. After the destruction of the temple, Leviticus might have been useful as a reminder of glories past, helping to retain in people's minds the freshness of the sacrificial cult and keep it alive. Perhaps it was useful as a historical record and as a code for preserving the immediate past, to reinforce hope for the restoration of the temple and the sacrificial system that was so valued.

To Jews at the beginning of the twenty-first century, Leviticus appears to be an uninspiring, esoteric, inaccessible text, not meaningful to people's lives. It does not appear reasonable as a basis for teaching the next generation. The Jewish community in the United States and elsewhere faces many challenges of religious identity and continuity, the quality of Judaism, the decline of religious observances and of Jewish education. Surely one might think there must be better texts to study and read, from which to learn the core of Jewish values. Indeed, some Jewish traditions have deemphasized this book of the Torah, dropping classic readings from it during High Holiday services when large crowds are in attendance.

In the United States, only a minority of Jews prays for the restoration of the animal sacrifice system in the land of Israel. Few pray for the return of the priests and Levites to conduct the temple service, slaughter animals, and sprinkle the blood on the altar. In their prayers for redemption, how much can American Jews be expected to link the restoration of Israel to the sacrificial cult of olden days? There are passages in the traditional prayer book that directly express hope for the restoration

of animal sacrifices. These have been altered in the regular religious services in most congregations to reflect history ("this is how our ancestors
did this") rather than hope for the future. Orthodox prayer books have
retained selections that refer to the future restoration of animal sacrifices.
I suspect that many of those who participate in Orthodox prayer services do not recognize the meaning of the prayers, and few Orthodox believ-
ers would be prepared to reinstitute the sacrifice system today.

Few contemporary Jews see their ideals of Judaism connected to the
sacrificial system. Indeed, the publishers of the prayer books of the
Reform, Reconstructionist, and Conservative versions of Judaism have
edited out prayers advocating a return to the good old days of animal
sacrifices. At best, most committed Jews view the issue of animal
sacrifice as history, not as future—as an heirloom, not as a basis for the
living fountain of Judaism. The message appears to be, Put the book of
Leviticus in the museum with other historical relics, some of which we
are proud of as our past. Let us view it as a symbol of the "primitive"
origins of our ancestors, which we have overcome with our modern way
of life. It is not a book to be studied or used to convey the core values of
Judaism.

It is interesting that rabbinical Judaism has taken a very different view
of the book of Leviticus. A tradition based on one of the oldest midrashic
(homiletical and interpretive) books on Leviticus (Vayikra Rabbah) says
that children should begin their education with the study of this book
of the Torah:

> Rabbi Issi asks, 'Why do they start children's education with Torat
> Kohanim, the handbook of the priest, the book of Leviticus? It would make
> more sense for them to start with B'reshit, the Book of Genesis' [i.e., with
> stories].
>
> An answer comes from God: Said the Holy One, Blessed be He, since
> the sacrifices are pure and the children are pure, let the pure come and
> engage in the study of the pure.

But there is more to the sacrifices than purity, as we shall see, and children are hardly pure, as we all know.

I had for many years been puzzled by that midrash, and as a student

in a traditional yeshiva I found study of the book of Leviticus less interesting and less relevant to my Judaism than other sections of the Torah.
I never fully appreciated the profound importance of Leviticus until I
thought of it as a basis for instruction about today and the future rather
than as a basis for understanding the past. To make Leviticus relevant
is to specify some of the fundamentals of Judaism and Jewish values.
Let me explain.

If we study the text of Leviticus carefully and thoughtfully as a religious text and not as a handbook (and not contextualized as a text of its
time), we can discern more clearly the core elements in Judaism. As a
result, we can infer relevance to contemporary Jewish communities.
Leviticus should not be read as apologetics or as a rationale for the animal sacrifices of another time—that is, other people conducted animal
sacrifices, too, but Jews did it more humanely. The Torah, including
Leviticus, is a basis for rethinking our understanding of contemporary
Jewish communities and their futures. Leviticus can be viewed as a living lesson in Judaic values.[4]

What are the core messages that Leviticus teaches about animal
sacrifices? I want to emphasize three (although there are many others
as well). First, some of the animal sacrifices (the *olah,* the *mincha,* and
the *shelomin*) are spontaneously motivated. They are not fixed by the calendar on fasts or feasts, Shabbat or holidays. They are not required offer-
ings but voluntary ones. The donor of the sacrifice does not give the
animal to the priest to prepare but takes an active role in the ritual. The
donor presents the animal, lays his hands on it, slaughters it, skins it,
and cuts it. Only in relation to the altar does the *kohen,* the priest, get
involved. (I am focusing here on Leviticus chapter 1. Other texts differ
slightly, but my point is the same.)

So the first message is that the Jewish community welcomes not only
required ritual but also spontaneous, voluntary action. The voluntary
activity, however, must be carried out within a community and within
patterns recognized by it. There is little room in this Judaism for pas-
sivity or private altars. Nor is the ritual anything that one may make up
spontaneously. The first set of lessons about participation emphasizes
voluntarism, community, and public involvement. The ritual links the
individual to the community. Animals were worth a lot in those days,

so the financial contribution of these sacrifices should not be minimized. The message: Volunteer generously to be part of the community.

The most important point about this lesson is the centrality of voluntarism, community, and public involvement as Jewish values. To the extent that we want to assess the continuity and cohesion of Jewish communities, we should be examining these features as they exist today. Researchers rarely assess Jewish communities using this set of values as a standard.

Second, one of the sacrifices the Torah describes is that conducted after a woman gives birth or after someone is healed of an illness (Lev. 12). Note that there are even egalitarian lessons to be learned from the Tanach: the same offering is designed for the birth of either a boy or a girl and for either a man or a woman who is healed. The healed person brings an animal to sacrifice as a *transition* back to the community from birth or illness. If one cannot afford a sheep, then one can bring two doves. There is no need for expensive gifts, the Torah teaches; no need for cattle. If one cannot afford to participate in some ways but still wants voluntarily to be part of the community, then social class and money should not be a barrier. One of the voluntary gifts that the Torah describes is the *qarbon mincha*, an exclusively cereal offering of grain and flour. This "sacrifice," or tribute to God, should reflect the fruit of one's labor. More importantly, this *mincha* is the poor person's animal sacrifice.[5] Wealth is not the key to community. All can participate; all can be involved. No stigma should be placed on those who have fewer resources or who are different. Caste and birth play no role in the system of voluntary contributions to the community. Everyone can contribute, not just the elites, the wealthy, or the *kohanim*.

Thus Leviticus not only teaches tolerance of the many but also institutionalizes a range of sacrifices, so that everyone can be included. This translates into the value of full participation by all members of the community. No one is godlike, though everyone is holy. That is the second lesson of the animal sacrificial system for Jewish communities. Diversity within the community needs to be incorporated, not merely tolerated. When everyone has the option and opportunity to be included, the community is most powerful. The incorporation of diversity is another part of this message for community development and values.

A third set of lessons from the discussions of animal sacrifice in Leviticus revolves around the issue of intent. The ritual of animal sacrifice means nothing in its abstract form. Animal sacrifice has no magic and no formal power. It remains simply animal sacrifice—primitive and magical (i.e., not Jewish)—until there is intent.

Intention transforms the mundane, ordinary, and secular into the holy and sacred. The process of *kedusha,* or sanctification of the mundane, takes what is prevalent in everyday culture and incorporates it within the system of Judaism. That is the core notion associated with animal sacrifices. The religious lesson is that Judaism must take from the cultural and real experiences of people's lives and transform them to make them Jewish. For the ancient Israelites, animals and agricultural production were central to daily life. The Torah teaches Jews to sanctify the routine and the everyday. The goal is to transform the ordinary to make it part of Jewish culture and values, even as Jews' everyday lives have changed radically over the centuries. Moreover, the integration of elements from surrounding cultures preserves rather than threatens Judaism and Jewish culture. In this sense, contemporary Jews should embrace the assimilation of "foreign" cultural themes into Judaic life, as their ancestors did in the past.

Sanctifying the mundane requires several steps, so the Torah teaches. One needs first to distinguish between the holy and the profane—*l'havdil ben kodesh l'chol.* But separation is not enough. To separate or to differentiate requires a new form of integration. Because one has to move between the profane and the sacred, one cannot build walls between them.

Sanctification takes place through the will and intent of individuals, but that is not enough. If it were only a matter of the will of individuals, then there would be no public ritual, no form, but instead religious anarchy. There would be no history, no continuity. Anyone could bring to the temple in Jerusalem whatever he wanted, whenever he wanted it, prepared in his own way. But the Torah teaches order and form, structure and specificity. One must bring certain things and not others, prepared in a particular way, to a certain place at a certain time. What the ritual adds up to is structure and continuity and at the same time the integration (i.e., sanctification) of the new. Continuity and integration require organizations and institutions. Again, the Torah emphasizes spontaneity, but within a community. It encourages individual intent, but within established institutions linked together to reach a level of religious expression.

Sanctification, then, occurs via the intention of the individual within a context of collective activity and organizational structure. The form in which sanctification takes place in the Torah is animal sacrifice, but the form itself is not the key part of the message of Jewish values. The message is what the Torah teaches about the *process* of sanctification and the values surrounding it, so that when new forms emerge, Jews know how to sanctify them and incorporate them within the Judaic system. When the rabbis replaced the sacrificial system with prayer, they linked individual intent, community, and the structure of ritual as parts of that transformation. The transformation makes the synagogue a special case within a general process.

Note that this message from the Torah about the value of assimilating from one's environment and sanctifying that which is assimilated— that is, making it one's own—rejects in the most fundamental sense withdrawal from the community, isolation from reality, and the performance of meaningless rituals that have no human intent. The Torah teaches the incorporation of the mundane, not its rejection. The message is to live in this world, not to withdraw from it. It encourages the linkage of the individual to the community through connections to others and institutions, all within a pattern established by tradition and consensus. And in the most profound and challenging sense, the message is that Jews should build on the new and incorporate it into the established community.

What wonderful lessons for Jews to teach their children when they are first learning about Jewish values. What wonderful lessons for adults to relearn themselves. Treating Judaism and Jewish values in their sociological and theological contexts, we can see that Judaism as a religion provides the opportunity for assimilating from the environment and thereby sanctifying the environment. Judaism involves intent and spontaneity, not just on the part of individuals but within a context of structure and community. Judaism is for everyone: diversity is to be incorporated in the community, not merely tolerated. Birth, wealth, and caste are not the keys to inclusion; commitment and involvement are. These are the challenges for the next generation, the future of the Jewish community. If we are to assess the Jewish values of a community, if we are to go beyond the numbers to reveal the values of Jewish continuity and to incorporate change, then we must search for those core values that are the heart of the Judaic system.

In this chapter and the preceding one, I have stressed context and community as sources of Judaic values. First, Shmuel Braw teaches us that although Jewish values and conceptions of the future change over the generations, Jewish culture can be adapted in new settings to achieve continuity. Second, the rabbinic conception of the prophet is that of a teacher, not a futurist or seer. The role of the prophet lies in the community, teaching core values to future generations. Third, the Torah, in its presentation of animal sacrifices, is not obsessed about the *forms* in which values are expressed. Rather, it teaches the centrality of institutions and communal commitments, the importance of ritual and participation by all, and the value of integrating new cultural forms Jewishly.

Putting these three themes together, we have a basis for understanding the centrality of Jewish values in shaping the Jewish future. These are lessons to teach children when they are first learning about Jewish values. They are wonderful lessons of culture and Judaism that can form the basis of Jewish cultural life in the future. Jews have not only stories about the past, not only the myths in Genesis and the histories in Exodus, but a combination of history, myth, story, and institutions in Leviticus. The challenge is to learn about these rich cultural traditions to make Judaism and Jewish communities attractive to those who seek to become Jewish and those who are Jewish by inheritance.

6

SECULARISM, RELIGION,

ETHNICITY, AND ASSIMILATION

Observers and analysts of the Jewish community have constructed three flawed but compelling arguments about the Jewish past and present that inform forecasts of the future. These arguments have been based, in part, on social science theories, and they have gained legitimacy in Jewish communities in the United States and elsewhere around the world as a basis for policy formation, research agendas, and strategic planning. They are also consistent with a set of ideological orientations that have been current among Jews for more than a century. Somewhat oversimplified, the three arguments are as follows.

First, Jewish communities have, over the last century, moved away from a foundation in religion and religious activities and toward secularism. In modern, open, voluntary societies, Jews, like others, have become more secular, less attached to religious activities and institutions and to a religious way of life. Whatever religious orientations their grandparents and great-grandparents had, contemporary Jews have fewer of them. Religion is simply less central in their lives today, it is argued. Judaism itself, with its associated religious institutions, has become more secular. Therefore, even those who are religiously committed today are more secular than their forebears were. This is the so-called secularization theme. It has been applied to all communities of Jews, both inside and outside of Israel.

The second argument focuses on the ethnic, or "peoplehood," dimension of Jewish identity. Jews in the past, so the argument goes, had a distinct sense of being a people apart from the Christians and Muslims among whom they lived. That is, they were a social minority, not only a religious one. Their minority status reduced their access to social and economic opportunities and involved political constraints and discrimination in everyday life, at times to extreme levels. However, with the increasing openness of society, the expansion of political rights, citizenship, and economic opportunities, and the increasing acceptance of Jews into society, the ethnic component of Jewishness has diminished. Like other white social minorities subject to decreasing discrimination, over the generations Jews have assimilated ethnically into Western societies. They have accepted their new situation and have been accepted by others. As generational distance from immigrant origins has increased—fewer and fewer American Jews have grandparents who experienced life outside the United States—the ethnic distinctiveness of American Jews has faded. Jews have become thoroughly American (or European) as the Jewish ethnic component of their lives has receded.

In Israel, Jews remain distinctive because they are different from their surrounding Arab neighbors. As Jews there have become increasingly "Israeli," they have also become decreasingly ethnic in terms of identification with their national origins. The Jews of Israel have thus become the quintessential ethnic national community, substituting "Israel" for specific nations of origin. The second argument suggests that when Jews are a minority in an open society, ethnic identity recedes and ethnic assimilation occurs over time. Only where Jews are a majority does ethnic or national identity become reinforced. But that identity can in turn become insignificant as a new national identity emerges, as in the case of Israel.

The third argument follows directly from and combines the secularization and minority assimilation arguments. It assumes that as religious identity weakens and ethnic identity fades, the cohesiveness of Jewish communities outside the State of Israel also weakens. External stimuli are therefore needed to ignite the dying embers of Jewishness. These sparks might come from a cultural attachment to and pride in the new nation-state, Israel, or from a recognition of Jewish vulnerability to external forces that threaten group survival. In their anti-Semitic and anti-Israel guises, these external factors tend to be unpredictable and to remain marginal to the daily lives of most Jews outside of Israel. They appear and reappear occasionally (particularly in Europe), almost always in reaction to events and conflicts in Israel. Thus, as secularization diminishes Judaism and assimilation weakens Jewish ethnicity, few internally generated Jewish values or features of Jewish culture remain to sustain the continuity of the community or of Jewish identity. As Judaism and Jewishness fade, so the argument goes, nothing beyond externals (e.g., anti-Semitic threats or pride in Israel) can undergird the future viability of Jewish communities outside of Israel.

In Israel, this third argument maintains, only Jews' sense of peoplehood maintains their group identity and distinctiveness. Secularization has become dominant for the majority of Jews in Israel, and secular Jews and the religious Orthodox have, for political, economic, and cultural reasons, become competitive with and often openly hostile to one another. The cultural component of Jewish identity in Israel is diminished by the powerful influences of mass media and Western culture. Nationalism, too, weakens as statehood is legitimated, routinized, and normalized, except in times of external threats and conflicts. (Indeed, some have argued that the Arab-Israeli conflict unifies Israeli Jews, for without the external enemy, Israel would be an even more ethnically divided society.) As Israeli Jewish national origins diminish over time, a new Israeli Jewish culture emerges that is highly selective in its historical memory and about its rich cultural heritage. Israeli Jewish culture tends to emphasize the biblical roots of nationalism, often ignoring the Judaisms of the rabbinic period and the richness of Diaspora cultural developments. The Jewish cultural cement of group life is therefore weakening in Israel, and cohesiveness is now sustained largely by historical reconstructions of external evil and internal survival.

These three arguments about secularization, assimilation, and cultural distinctiveness have in one form or another shaped recent discussions of Jewish futures inside and outside of Israel. Some social scientists and historians believe that Jewish communities outside of Israel are eroding and the Jewish Diaspora is vanishing. The decline of Jewish communities is in sight—if not in the present generation, then soon. The demographic strength of Jewish communities in Israel is offset by their cultural and ethnic decline and their political conflicts and weaknesses.

A systematic body of evidence, I submit, challenges these arguments, which do not adequately describe the paths Jewish communities have taken in modern, open, pluralistic societies. Although Jews have clearly assimilated, their communities have not always been proportionately weakened, and many have been strengthened anew. The fundamental dichotomy between religious and ethnic identity is not as useful among Jews as it may be among other groups. Because of their ethnic identity and culture, Jews are not simply a religious group like Protestants and Catholics, Mormons and Muslims. Because of their religious culture, Jewish Americans are not simply an ethnic group like Italian Americans or Hispanic Americans. And although Israeli Jews have developed common nationalistic commitments, their ethnic identities and communities also divide them. In large part, the ethnic and religious differences seen today in Israel were created in Israel itself, rather than having been transferred from places of origin.[1]

The distinctions between religious and secular identities are also unclear, since Judaism readily incorporates the secular. Empirically, there are multiple links between religious and ethnic secular indicators of Jewishness, although Judaism and ethnicity are not identical. The distinction between religious and secular, or between ethnic and religious, does not neatly distinguish among institutions of the community. Synagogues and temples have diversified their activities to incorporate strong ethnic components, and secular Jewish institutions have often stressed sacred themes.[2] So the survival paradigms, the dichotomies of ethnicity versus religion, minority versus majority, are not very useful as guidelines for studying contemporary Jewish communities, if they ever were in the past, and regardless of their utility for studying other groups.

How can we make sense of the historical changes in Jewish communities and their implications for the future? How do we go beyond current arguments about decay that cloud our assessments of the future and achieve new understandings and therefore new visions for the future? How do we get beyond the cliches of social science, the nuances of assimilation versus transformation, the rhetoric of optimists versus pessimists that trivialize the basic issues? We should move away from the selective truths of Jewish ideology and Jewish organizational propaganda to delve more systematically into the fundamentals of Jewish continuity and change. In this chapter I move beyond the oversimplified demographic argument about numbers to assess the major forms of Jewish quality of life. As I argued in earlier chapters, the issues of the Jewish future are mainly associated with such quality. I start with and focus on the United States, which has the largest Jewish community in the world.

AMERICAN JEWISH DISTINCTIVENESS

Instead of asking whether the grandchildren and great-grandchildren of eastern European Jewish immigrants to the United States are assimilating or whether they are surviving as a community (they are doing both), some social scientists have reformulated the central analytic questions about Jews and other ethnic and religious minorities in the United States. They now ask, What factors sustain the ethnic and religious distinctiveness of American Jews in the absence of overt discrimination and disadvantage? What structural and cultural forces sustain continuity in the face of pressures toward the disintegration of the uniqueness and distinctiveness of their communities? The short answer is that communal institutions and social and family networks are the core elements sustaining communal continuity and distinctiveness. Institutions are able to construct new forms of Jewish cultural uniqueness that redefine the collective identity of American Jews. Jewish values are the sources of continuity and are anchored in the structural underpinnings of communities.

Three features of social life form the basis for my assessment of the transformation of American Jews. First, I focus on the structural features of Jewish communities, not only on the cultural ones. Second, I emphasize the contexts (networks and institutions), not only the values, that distinguish Jews from others. Third, I target communities and families rather than individuals as the units of analysis and interpretation. To assess the formation and development of the community over time, I argue that we need to examine the quality of Jewish communal life in its broadest meaning. With the emergence of the fourth and later generations, distance from immigrant origins has faded as the major axis of change in the community. Although individuals exit and enter the community, its institutions and collectively shaped culture sustain ethnic continuity and commitments.

Social class and family patterns in American Jewish communities are the core of generational continuity, and institutions are the sources of distinctiveness. Jews have been transformed from an immigrant group defined by a combination of religion and ethnicity to an American ethnic community defined by a distinctive cultural construction of Judaism and Jewishness with central features that are particularly American. This transformation makes historical comparisons by generation problematical, and cross-national comparisons using similar indicators of continuity, distorting. I argue for the importance of context and structure in shaping comparisons over time. Changes over the life course as families are reformed and expand are the bases for exploring group distinctiveness in a wide variety of social spheres.

Several analytic themes shape my orientation. First, changes over time in the characteristics of Jews and their communities do not necessarily imply the decline of community or the total assimilation of Jews. The identification of changes over time may imply the transforming of community but not its disintegration. Second, my focus is on the cohesion of communities, based on the extent and contexts of intra- and intergroup interaction along with a shared, constructed (and often changing) culture. Sharing and interaction may occur in specific institutional or religious contexts but are likely to occur in the daily round of activities associated with the multiple spheres of social life—work, school, neighborhood, leisure, and family. Nevertheless, an examination of interaction in any one sphere may not have implications for interaction in other spheres. Third, time can be viewed both in terms of generations—that is, as historical context—and in terms of the life course. I expect that ethnic and religious identity, at both the individual and communal levels, varies over time as context changes. The life course is one perspective at the micro-level for studying a variety of unfolding and emerging changes in ethnic communities.

A wide variety of structural and institutional features links American Jews to one another in complex networks and marks them off as a community from people who are not Jewish. These features include family and social connections, organizational, political, and residential patterns, and religious and ethnic activities that can reinforce values and shape attitudes. I review some of these core features to identify their role in the integration of Jews into American society. At the outset, let me reiterate that institutions play a powerful role in ethnic communities for two reasons: they continually construct the cultural basis of community, and they represent the conspicuous, communal, public symbols of community.

Family and social networks reinforce shared cultural constructions of Judaism and Jewishness. Declines or increases in any one of the social spheres do not necessarily imply similar changes in all spheres. Evidence of a generational decline in organizational participation or synagogue attendance, for example, does not necessarily mean the decline of other forms of communal activities. Low levels of communal commitment at some stages of the life course do not necessarily imply continuing low levels at other stages. We need an examination of all the social processes over time (and over the life course) for an assessment of future directions in the transformation of the Jewish community.

Immigration to the United States

There are many entry points to the analysis of the future of the American Jewish community. I begin with a review of its formation and the role immigration played in that process at the turn of the twentieth century. The historical context provides the basis for understanding the roots of the community, the routes immigrants and their children have taken out of the community, and the transformations they have experienced. I also note some of the distortions that have characterized our understanding of the immigration and integration processes of American Jews. I then turn to the major changes in quality of life that have characterized the contemporary American Jewish community, including its changing educational, occupational, and family patterns, and conclude with some notes about the importance of social networks and institutions. The goal is to view the past as part of an assessment of the future trajectory of the American Jewish community.

Immigration to the United States from the countries of eastern Europe, beginning in the 1870s and continuing through the 1920s, became the demographic foundation of the contemporary American Jewish community. Drawing on significant proportions of Jewish communities of origin, the immigration involved 2.5 million Jews, mostly from towns and urban areas. It was a collective and voluntary migration, reflecting the push of economic and political constraints in places of origin and the pull of opportunities in places of destination. In turn, powerful kinship networks facilitated the attractiveness of the United States.

Social and ideological changes had already affected immigrants and their communities before they left, resulting in the immigrants' greater receptivity to the range of opportunities available in the United States. Many Jews in eastern Europe, particularly those who decided to immigrate to America, already had experienced increases in education, were engaged in urban occupations, and had been exposed to secular, nationalist, and socialist ideologies and organizations. They fit in with the expanding urban industrial economy, the emphasis on public education, and the challenges of social mobility characteristic of the early twentieth-century United States. Immigrant Jews embraced the American dream. A combination of the immigrants' urban social and economic background, American economic opportunity, the volume and characteristics of immigration, the role of kinship networks, and the presence of other ethnic and religious groups in the broader immigration stream shaped the nature of the first generation of American Jews from eastern Europe.

The volume of immigration and the distribution of immigrants transformed the scattered local American Jewish communities into a national ethnic group, raising the Jewish population in the United States from 200,000 in 1870 to over 4 million in the mid-1920s. The guiding ideology of this immigration from eastern Europe was secular-socialist, not religious. An ethnic Jewish identity in the broadest sense, not a narrowly defined Judaism, characterized the immigrant community. The economic motives underlying the immigration were dominant (an escape from economic discrimination and oppression, not only fear of pogroms); the immigrants' capitalist goal was to take advantage of the economic opportunities (grounded in political opportunities) that were available in the United States. Socialism was their politics; capitalism was their economics; Jewishness was their social and family life and their culture.

The heaviest Jewish immigration from eastern Europe occurred between 1904 and 1908, when 650,000 Jews arrived, and in 1913–14, when an additional quarter of a million arrived. In no year, however, was Jewish immigration more than 14 percent of general immigration, and more often than not it was less than 10 percent. Aided by local and national Jewish American organizations, informed by extended family members and persons from their towns of origin, the overwhelming majority of Jews remained in the United States, arriving with family members or bringing them in subsequent years. This permanent, family- and community-based immigration made it reasonable for Jews to invest in learning English, forming new families, and financing the education of their children. With little or no incentive to return to their places of origin, with economic opportunities available, and with financial assistance from earlier Jewish immigrants from Germany, Jews from eastern Europe became citizens in their new homeland. They competed well with the millions of other immigrants who were less well prepared because of their more rural origins and lesser commitment to remaining in the United States.[3]

In order to assess the impact of the receiving society on Jewish immigrants, we need first to identify immigrant self-selection. Not all Jews came to the United States, even when few restrictions were placed on immigration from eastern Europe. Indeed, most Jews remained in eastern Europe, and Jewish population size there continued to increase rapidly during the period of mass emigration. As in other migrations, younger adults were more likely to move and were selective about where they went on socioeconomic grounds. Property owners and those with good jobs (like Shmuel Braw as described in chapter 4) were least likely to migrate. The poorest and the least educated were also unlikely to have the resources to move. A much higher proportion of skilled laborers and a much lower proportion of unskilled workers were to be found among the immigrants than among the Jewish labor force in eastern Europe. Pressures to move were greatest in urban areas where Jews were squeezed during the early period of industrialization. Emigration attracted those whose skills were most transportable. As in other migrations, those most receptive to change were already somewhat freed from the constraints of family and tradition and had already experienced some social and economic mobility. Ironically, through emigration Jews were becoming more independent of their families while at the same time families were developing bonds of assistance and support for immigration and assimilation. Independence did not mean the rejection of family ties but resulted in the establishment of new forms of kinship bonds and family support.

Most of the religious leaders and their closest followers remained in eastern Europe. They correctly viewed the United States as threatening to their authority and their religious traditions. But whereas they labeled America the *trayfa medena*, the "unfit country," the socialists and secularists, who were disproportionately numerous among the immigrants, saw the United States as the "golden land" or the "promised land." The immigrants brought with them the cultural societies, unions, and political parties of eastern European Jewry, leaving behind most of the religious institutions, including the religious educational ones.

Few Jewish immigrants severed their ties to their places of origin, even as they became American. Kinship and friendship ties were the bases of further immigration of relatives and friends from communities of origin. Chain migration, not return migration, was a dominant feature of eastern European Jewish immigration to the United States. International ties with extended family and neighbors developed among Jewish immigrants, shaping networks of support and interaction among them and their children. Settlement and organizational patterns in the United States reinforced ties to communities of origin. Building religious and welfare institutions, coming from the same region, and living close together in neighborhoods, immigrants conveyed to their children the sense of community and culture of their places of origins, including the depths of their Jewish identification. By the first and second decades of the twentieth century, thousands of independent *landsmanschaften* (organizations based on communities of origin) and other local immigrant organizations existed in American cities where Jews were concentrated.

The immigrant generation was residentially concentrated in particular neighborhoods in a few large cities, dominated by New York. By

1920 almost half the Jews in the United States lived in New York, and almost two-thirds lived in only three states. Almost 85 percent were concentrated in cities of 100,000 or more, in comparison with less than 30 percent of the total population. Only 3 percent lived in rural areas, in comparison with 46 percent of the total. The economic activities of Jewish immigrants distinguished them from those they left behind in places of origin and from other immigrants. The overwhelming concentration of immigrant Jews in skilled labor provided Jews with enormous structural advantages over other immigrants in the pursuit of occupational integration and social mobility. A distinct overlap of ethnicity and occupation emerged among Jewish immigrants, and powerful economic networks, occupational niches, and occupational concentration developed.[4]

Their social and economic background, residential and occupational concentration, and family characteristics allowed immigrant Jews to take advantage of the expanding educational opportunities in the United States. Working in more skilled and stable occupations, Jews earned more money than did other immigrants. This facilitated investment in their children's education. Over time, the direction of the link between occupation and educational level reversed: those with better educations were able to obtain better jobs. But mobility away from neighborhoods of initial settlement and to new jobs and higher levels of education was manifested as a group process. Those who attended college, for example, were usually commuters who lived with their families at home. Jews tended to concentrate in certain schools as well. By 1920, more than 80 percent of the students enrolled in City College and Hunter College in New York were Jewish. Before Columbia University instituted restrictive quotas after World War I, 40 percent of its student enrollment was Jewish.[5]

The immigrant generation could not shed its Jewishness, but it could change it. The foreignness of the immigrant population, its structural and cultural characteristics, and the discrimination it encountered prevented or constrained its full assimilation. Residential, educational, and occupational networks joined family and organizational networks to reinforce a cohesive ethnic community. These bases of cohesion would inevitably change over time as the children of immigrants moved to new neighborhoods, attended different schools for longer periods of time, obtained better jobs, and faced the economic depression of the 1930s and war in the 1940s. Yet the children of immigrants were raised in cohesive, supportive families where an ethnic language was distinctive, where cultural closeness to origins was undeniable, and where networks and institutions were ethnically based. Together, these powerful elements made the second generation Jewish by both religion and ethnicity, in the sense of national origin. But that ethnicity was fading, and the second generation's Jewishness was becoming Americanized. Although sharply different from the Jewishness of their parents' generation, the children's Jewishness was clear and distinctive by American standards. The critical issue of change and continuity among Jewish Americans is initially a matter of closeness to foreign origins and length of time in American society. The continuation of integration into the third and fourth generations, distant from their cultural origins, raises the question of the changing quality of American Jewish life.

At work, in neighborhoods, in schools, and in religious, political, and social activities, immigrant Jews and their children were interacting with other Jews. Yiddish and socialist schools and newspapers competed with public and religious schools. Credit associations, *landsmanschaften,* and local fraternal and communal institutions appeared and expanded. Although people were learning English, Yiddish remained the language of business and social life among Jewish immigrants. Even when their children rejected Yiddish as their own language, it was still the cultural environment of their upbringing. In the pre-World War II period, most Jews in the United States interacted with other Jews in their community. And Jewish families and communities rejected those who rejected them through intermarriage or by their behavior. For most Jews, the number of bases of community cohesion was large indeed. The overlap of occupation, residence, and ethnicity among Jews was as high in the United States as anywhere in urban Europe. Jews left the Old World behind, but not all of it, to become American. Their Jewishness was conspicuous by their background, culture, and social structure.

Stratification and the Cohesion of Communities

What happened to the community and to ethnic and religious identity among the descendants of the immigrants? Clearly, the third and later generations faced a very different social and economic context. Shaping social and residential mobility across the generations was the role of the educational and occupational opportunity structure. In turn, stratification, or the concentration of Jews in particular social classes, became one of the key structural conditions affecting cohesion within Jewish communities in the United States. I therefore begin my review of the transformation of American Jews with the topic of stratification. I review the educational levels and occupations of Jews using evidence from U.S. censuses and sample surveys dating to 1910, 1970, and 1990. More recent data are not yet available from the National Jewish Population Survey of 2001, but it is unlikely that these data will disconfirm the major trends presented here.

Education. The story of the changing educational profile of the American Jewish community during the twentieth century is for the most part clear and well known. Jews in the United States have become the most highly educated of all American ethnic and religious groups, of all Jewish communities around the world, and of all Jewish communities ever in recorded Jewish history. This is quite a feat, given the low level of education of American Jews three to four generations ago. The accomplishment reflects both the value that Jews place on education and the educational opportunities available in the United States. Over 90 percent of American Jewish young men and women now go on to college, and they are the children of mothers and fathers who also studied in college. Many have grandparents who had exposure to some college education. Increases in the educational level of the American Jewish population have been documented in every study carried out over the last several decades, and the level attained is a distinguishing feature of American Jewish communities. It may be a core value of contemporary American Jewish culture.

National data sources allow us to analyze this dramatic change in detail. Using both the 1970 and 1990 National Jewish Population Surveys, along with comparable data on the non-Hispanic white population from U.S. census and Current Population Survey data, I constructed the educational attainment levels of American Jews born in the pre-1905 period and in subsequent cohorts through 1950–60. These cohorts show how school enrollment developed from the first decade of the twentieth century through the 1990s, since those born in the early part of the twentieth century completed their education by the 1920s, and those born in the 1950s and 1960s completed theirs by the 1980s and 1990s. The data highlight several important features of the educational transformation of American Jews.[6]

First, cohorts of Jewish men and women born before 1905 had relatively low levels of education, but over time educational levels increased, first for men and then for women. Viewing these cohorts as a single generation, we can conclude that Jewish men and women born in the first decade of the twentieth century had, on average, only primary and perhaps some secondary education. Those who completed high school were exceptional within the Jewish community, as well as among their non-Jewish age peers. In contrast, American Jews growing up at the end of the twentieth century are largely college graduates; those not completing college have become clear exceptions. Jews born in the 1920s and 1930s were much more heterogeneous educationally than the cohorts born before or after them. These middle cohorts lived through a period of transition in the schooling of American Jews, a period when the rate of educational change and the choices about whether to continue schooling at various stages were at a maximum. The transition generation was also the generation of greatest tension between foreignness and American integration. Generational conflict was highly correlated with changing levels of educational attainment during this middle period.

These educational data refer to individuals, retrospectively constructed, with generational and compositional changes inferred. Cross-sectional views that are contemporary with the periods examined are powerful additional reminders of how the community appeared educationally at various points in time. The 1910 United States census provides a brief glimpse of educational patterns for Jews (defined as those whose mother tongue was Yiddish or who lived in households where Yiddish was spoken) and others. Data on literacy reveal lower levels among Jewish men than among others in 1910 and significantly lower levels among Jewish women than among either Jewish men or other women. So the educational starting point for Jews, most of whom were recent immigrants in 1910, was lower than for others. Estimates of school enrollment by age in 1910 suggest that Jewish children ages fourteen to eighteen were less likely to be in school than native whites and even some other immigrant groups. Jewish men who were born in the United States, however, had much higher enrollment levels and the highest estimated number of years of schooling completed.

Comparing national data on two cross sections of Jews and others in 1970 and 1990, data that encompass the variety of cohorts making up the American Jewish community at those points in time, confirms the educational transformation of Jews. By the end of the twentieth century Jews had become a community with distinctively high levels of education, higher than other groups in the United States. The overall increase in American educational levels over the last thirty years has only marginally reduced the gap between Jews and others. On the whole, the Jewish community has become concentrated at the upper end of the educational distribution, reducing the educational heterogeneity among Jews and thereby creating a new structural basis of community and commonality between generations.

Occupation. How have these educational patterns been translated into changing patterns of occupational concentration among men and women? The 1910 census data show that a majority of American Jews (again defined as those living in households where Yiddish was the mother tongue) were either skilled or semiskilled factory workers.[7] Few were professionals or managers. When Jews worked in white-collar jobs, they tended toward sales work. Jewish women with jobs outside the home in 1910 were also heavily concentrated in blue-collar work, and few held professional or managerial positions. At the beginning of the twentieth century, Jewish men and women were distinctive in their occupational concentration in sales and in factory work.

In the two generations born before 1970, the Jewish occupational pyramid was upended. It shifted from 55 percent of males in worker or service positions in 1910 to 69 percent in professional and managerial positions in 1970. For Jewish women with jobs, the pyramid shifted from 73 percent in worker or service categories in 1910 to 46 percent in professional and managerial jobs and 37 percent in clerical jobs in 1970.

Between 1970 and 1990, there was an increase in professional occupations among Jewish men and women along with a rather sharp decline (over 50 percent) in managerial positions among Jewish men.

These radical shifts in occupational structure over time have resulted in new forms of occupational distinctiveness for Jews in the United States, in comparison with white non-Hispanics in metropolitan areas. Particularly conspicuous is the greater concentration of Jews in professional jobs, which parallels their educational attainments. We can further compare the occupational concentration of Jews and non-Jews by using information on extent of self-employment, the specific jobs Jews hold within broad occupational categories, and the proportion of the total occupational distribution that is captured by a small number of jobs.

The 1910 census subdivides employment status into three categories: employer, own account, and working for wages. Not surprisingly, most everyone worked for wages in 1910—Jews and others, men and women. Nevertheless, Jewish men were much more likely to be self-employed or to be an employer than were others. One-third of the Jewish males who were working were self-employed, compared with 16 percent of the total population. Estimates from the 1970 and 1990 National Jewish Population Surveys suggest that the proportion of the self-employed declined among Jewish men between 1970 and 1990, from 38 percent to 32 percent. However, the level of self-employment remained high for Jewish men, and its pattern contrasted with that of the total population, which experienced an increase from 10 percent to 15 percent. Thus, despite some convergence in the level of self-employment between Jewish and other males, the Jewish level continued to be distinctive. Even as the level of self-employment remained higher among Jews, the meaning of self-employment radically changed. Not only do self-employed professionals and self-employed tailors require different levels of education, but their occupations are also likely to have different implications for ethnic networks and for generational transfers of skills.

The new forms of occupational concentration can be further observed by comparing shifts in specific jobs within broader occupational categories between 1910 and 1990. I regrouped the jobs that accounted for 50 percent of the total occupational distribution of Jews and calculated as well the percentage of the total population in these jobs. The data show that 50 percent of all Jewish men were concentrated in only six specific jobs in 1910, whereas the same jobs encompassed just over 11 percent of the total U.S. population. The concentration in skilled and semiskilled categories of work and also in specific jobs was even greater for Jewish women than for both Jewish men and the total population. More than half of Jewish working women in 1910 were found in only five jobs, whereas only 12 percent of the total female population held these jobs.

By 1970, some changes could be observed. Almost three out of ten Jewish men were now in managerial or administrator positions, compared with 7 percent of the non-Hispanic white population. Lawyers, accountants, and physicians comprised a disproportionate number of Jewish males, as did retail and wholesale sales jobs. In each case, job concentration in these areas was significantly greater for Jews than for the total white population. The overall range of specific jobs held by Jews had diversified by 1970, and the status of those jobs within the occupational hierarchy had risen. Jewish women were also concentrated in a limited number of jobs in 1970. Like most other women, they were disproportionately secretaries, with only small differences between them and non-Jewish white women. Compared with other women, however, significant numbers of Jewish women were now managers and administrators, schoolteachers at all grade levels, sales workers, and clerical workers other than secretaries. The much broader number of occupations characterizing Jewish men and women in 1970 than in 1910 reflected educational changes and the widening of occupational opportunities within the country as a whole and among Jews in particular as the American economy developed. Both occupational diversity and new types of occupational concentration had emerged among Jews by 1970.

These patterns continued through 1990. Again, examining particular jobs and the number of jobs that account for about half of all working Jews reveals a significantly longer list of occupations than in 1970 yet continuing occupational distinctiveness when Jews are compared with the total population. Comparing the 1970 and 1990 data shows a shift away from managerial positions toward both more specialized and new professional jobs. Where comparison with the non-Jewish occupational distribution is possible, the continued distinctiveness of the distribution of jobs among Jewish men becomes evident, even as the number of jobs making up half of the occupational structure increases. Moreover, the shift in jobs among Jewish women in the two decades before 1990 parallels that among Jewish men. Jewish women in the labor force moved out of secretarial work and into a greater diversity of jobs, including more professional positions, although the strong impression remains of continued gender segregation in the workplace, among Jews as among others.

Implications of Changing Stratification for Jewishness. What do these changes in education and occupation—that is, in stratification—imply for the continuity of the American Jewish community? There are two views. On one hand, increases in educational attainment and the diversification of occupational types result in greater interaction with non-Jewish "others." These new contexts of interaction between Jews and non-Jews challenged the earlier segregation of Jews and in turn challenge the cohesion of the Jewish community. In schools and workplaces, Jewish Americans may also be exposed to new networks and alternative values that are not ethnically or religiously Jewish. The combination of interaction and exposure may result in a diminishing of the distinctiveness of the community over time, through family changes and generational discontinuity. So the changes in stratification are associated with new intergroup interaction patterns that lead to diminished community cohesion.

A different interpretation of this picture is sometimes offered. That is, the emerging commonality of social class among Jews and the distinctiveness of Jews relative to others (assuming that some form of educational or occupational distinctiveness remains intact) are themselves important sources of cohesion for the Jewish community. Jews are both marked off from others and linked with other Jews by their resources, networks, and lifestyles. To the extent that community is based on both interaction among members and a common set of values and lifestyles, these occupational and educational transformations among American Jews suggest significantly stronger bases of communal cohesion than existed at mid-century, when there was greater educational and occupational heterogeneity. The mobility of Jews away from the occupations characteristic of the immigrant generation has been a dominant theme in research. Missing has been an emphasis on the new educational and occupational concentrations that have emerged.

These two alternative outcomes of the educational and occupational transformations that Jews experienced in twentieth-century America are often presented in oversimplified and extreme forms. Clearly, American Jews cannot be characterized as either totally assimilated (in the sense of loss of communal cohesion) or as an isolated, entirely cohesive community. There should be more direct ways than by inference to assess the effects of stratification changes on the quality of Jewish life. Researchers have reached no consensus, however, about how or even what to measure to reveal the quality of Jewish life in the United States. Nor does sufficient evidence exist about the nature and implications of the educational and occupational networks that Jews have developed over the life course and generationally. Consequently, the emerging balance of Jewish communal life and its linkage to the educational and occupational changes experienced by Jews cannot be fully assessed.

Nonetheless, national data on selected aspects of Jewish life can be linked to the educational and occupational patterns I have outlined. A review of some analytical explorations along these lines is suggestive.[8] Measures of Jewishness that tapped the ethnic and religious expressions of Jews in 1990—including seasonal ritual observances (Passover and Hanukkah), traditional rituals (kashrut and Shabbat observances), participation in Jewish educational and organizational activities, associational ties (Jewish friends and neighbors), philanthropy (contributions to Jewish charities), and attitudes about intermarriage—were related statistically to the occupational and educational characteristics of households. Not surprisingly, the results were complex, but three of them are revealing.

First, many of the education and occupation measures were not directly related to indicators of Jewishness. Jewishness reflects the family life course (e.g., age, family structure, presence and ages of children) rather than educational or occupational attainment. Occupational measures were only weakly related to most of the Jewishness factors that were examined. It appears that the commonality of jobs and self-employment are not directly linked with religious and most ethnic ties. These data are consistent with the argument that occupational concentration and

related measures have altered over the generations and that the implications of these factors for Jewish continuity may thus also have changed.
In the past, occupational mobility and educational attainment were linked
to disaffection from the ethnic community. That is no longer the case.
The absence of a relationship between occupation and measures of
Jewishness may also imply that having these occupational ties is an important basis for Jewish interaction and Jewish networks. If occupational
networks substitute for Jewish communal and religious networks, then
we should expect that the relationship between occupational concentration and measures of Jewishness would be weak. There are no measures of ethnic economic resources, ethnic networks, and ethnic business
connections with which to test these arguments directly.

The situation is somewhat clearer for education. Using several indicators of education, the evidence shows that higher levels of education
reinforce and strengthen Jewish expressions, particularly those that are
tied to participation in Jewish communal activities. College education
seems to promote Jewish-related activities for the age group below forty-
five; this is less the case for older cohorts. In this sense, the negative
relationship between attending college and Jewishness in the past had
changed significantly by the 1990s. This is consistent with the view that
the Jewish alienation presumed to be associated with higher levels of
education occurs when higher education is the exception, characteristic of the few. When exposure to college and university education is almost
universal, its impact on Jewishness becomes minimal or is reversed.[9]

Finally, there is no systematic evidence that the changed stratification
profile of the American Jewish community results in Jews' abandoning
the community in terms of the wide range of Jewish expressions. There
is no systematic relationship between, on the one hand, becoming a professional, working for others, or being in a job where there are few Jews
and, on the other hand, most, if not all, of the measures of Judaic expression, either as individual measures or as part of a general Jewishness index.

Contexts of Assimilation

The evidence points to the conclusion that neither high levels of education nor concentration in managerial and professional jobs weakens

the intensity of Jewishness in all its multifaceted expressions. To be sure, the commonality of social class among American Jews, their educational attainment, and their occupational reconcentration are not likely to be sufficient to generate the intensive in-group interaction that character- ized the segregated Jewish communities in some parts of eastern Europe and the United States a century ago. The benefits of these trans- formations in terms of networks and resources have not re-created the cultural and social communities of Jews of a different era. Nevertheless, and this is the critical point, the evidence indicates that the emerging social class patterns are not a threat to Jewish continuity in the trans- formed pluralism of American society.

The educational and occupational transformations of twentieth- century America clearly mark Jews off from others and connect Jews to one another. The connections among persons who share history and experience and their separation from others are what social scientists refer to as community. The distinctiveness of the American Jewish com- munity in these stratification patterns has become sharper.

When these stratification profiles are added to the picture of residential concentration of American Jews, the community features become even sharper. Many have noted the move away from areas of immigrant res- idential concentration, the residential dispersal of American Jews, and the shaping of new forms of residential concentration for the second and later generations. Some of these new forms involve the development of Jewish neighborhoods in large urban areas; others involve middle and upper middle-class suburban areas with large Jewish populations. Regional concentrations of Jews in the southern and western United States have also emerged; these tend to be smaller than concentrations in the northeast, but they, too, encourage interaction among Jews. Some places are not characterized by "Jewish" residential neighborhoods but by Jewish networks that have developed around schools, country clubs, organizations, and religious institutions that reinforce interaction and ethnic culture. And even newer forms of "virtual" interaction have emerged with Internet connections among family and friends. The occu- pational concentration of Jews, attendance at selected schools and col- leges, and work in selected metropolitan areas have resulted in powerful new forms of networks and institutions. The geographic concentration

of American Jews is astonishing for a voluntary ethnic white group several generations removed from foreignness and not facing the discrimination experienced by other American minorities.

The value placed by Jews on educational attainment as a mechanism
for becoming American (and obtaining good jobs and earning higher
incomes) is clearly manifested in the context of the opportunities open
to Jews in the United States. Their higher level of education and their
concentration in professional and managerial jobs has not led to the "erosion" or total assimilation of the Jewish community. While these changes
may have resulted in the disaffection of some individual Jews from the
community, they may also have resulted in the greater incorporation
within the Jewish community of some who were not born Jewish, increasing the general attractiveness of the community to Jews and to others.

Educational, residential, and occupational concentration implies not
only cohesion and lifestyle similarity among Jews but also exposure to
options for integration and assimilation. Education implies exposure to
conditions and cultures that are more universal and less ethnically based,
even when most Jews are sharing this experience and are heavily concentrated in certain colleges and universities. If high levels of educational attainment and occupational achievement enhance the choices
that Jews make about their Jewishness, then Jewish identification and
intensity of Jewish expression are becoming increasingly voluntary in
twenty-first-century America. In that sense, the new forms of American
Jewish stratification have beneficial implications for the quality of
Jewish life. A balance exists between the forces that pull Jews toward
each other, toward sharing what we call community—families, experiences, history, concerns, values, communal institutions, religious rituals and commitments, and lifestyles—and those that pull Jews away from
each other, forces often referred to as "assimilation." The available evidence suggests that the pulls and pushes of the changing stratification
profile toward and away from the Jewish community are profound. They
are positive in strengthening the community, and they represent a challenge for institutions in terms of finding ways to reinforce their communal and cultural benefits.

Education has become one of the core values of contemporary
American Jewish culture and in the past was a powerful path toward social

mobility. Education led to better jobs, higher incomes, escape from the poverty of the immigrants' unskilled and skilled labor, and escape from the neighborhoods and networks of the foreign born. Education was a means of escape from the association of foreignness with a foreign language, a foreign culture, and foreign parents. For many, education was the escape from Jewishness and Judaism. In short, education was the path to becoming American, but it required leaving the community.

Education has almost always been celebrated among Jews, and pride has been taken in the group's accomplishments. When children and grandchildren became doctors and lawyers, skilled businesspeople and teachers, it was thought that this was the "Jewish" thing to do. But in those early years there was a cost. The cost was for Judaism and Jewishness and more importantly for relationships between the generations. Although parents encouraged their children to obtain a high level of education, the lifestyle associated with higher education often meant disruption and conflict between parents and children who had different educational levels and between siblings and peers who had different access to educational opportunities.

But looking beyond the costs, American Jews now appreciate the value of education over the last two generations. The value of education has not lessened, but the opportunities have increased and spread. Education has not disrupted Jewishness but has increased generational similarities and removed one source of the generation gap. So the meaning of two generations of college-educated Jews becomes not simply a note of group congratulations and pride, not only a changed relationship to Jewishness as a basis of intergenerational commonality. Educational attainment has become a feature of families that is not disruptive of them and that points to increasingly shared common experiences.

An analysis of the educational attainment of American Jews, then, points to the increased power of families, the generational increase in resources, and the common lifestyles that, far from dividing families, bind parents and children together in a network of relationships. These emphases on education and achievement, on family cohesion and values, have become group traits that make Jewishness attractive to others. Unlike in the past, when interaction and even marriage between

Jews and non-Jews could be a mechanism of escape from Jewishness and foreignness, the Jewish group has now become attractive to others because of its family and communal traits—particularly, but not solely, its emphasis on education. By binding the generations, education has become a family value.

The Content of American Jewishness: Religion and Religiosity

What about the content of this generational commonality? What are families sharing Jewishly? Are they sharing Jewish culture and Judaism? Let us do a brief mental exercise. Think about the meaning of Judaism two hundred years ago in parts of eastern Europe, where the majority of Jews in the world lived. Let us consider a social scientist who decides to take a survey of these communities. Under the financial constraints of the Jewish organizational sponsor and under pressure from local rabbis, the researcher includes questions about synagogue membership, the frequency of attendance at religious services, and the extent of Jewish education as indicators of religiosity. In carrying out the statistical analysis of this survey, the social scientist is surprised by the following findings: Almost no women attend synagogue services (except in a few large cities), and then only a few times a year. Few boys past the age of bar mitzvah, and even fewer girls of any age, have any Jewish education. Neither have their parents. Many men do not attend services regularly because, living in communities where there are few Jews, they do not have a minyan, or quorum of ten adult men. More likely, they attend services a few times a year when they are able to come to a large town, where there are more Jews, and stay with extended relatives. The social scientist excluded questions about studying religious texts or knowledge of religious rituals, because no one expected the frequencies to be high.

Though almost all the synagogues in our imagined community of two hundred years ago are filled with worshipers, not all people are able to attend daily or weekly services, either because they live too far from a synagogue or, again, because they have no quorum of adult males. Many Jews at this time in eastern Europe live in places where there are few synagogues, few Jews, and no Jewish institutions. Most of them are busy with the difficult task of surviving economically, a task that takes up most of their time and energy. Few have a formal Jewish education or provide one for their children.

Our social scientist is able to make some further observations. The bitter cold of late fall in rural eastern Europe and the absence of transportation mean that other rituals in the annual Jewish calendar, such as building a sukkah and purchasing one's own *lulav* or *etrog* for the Sukkot holiday, are neglected. They are simply out of reach for most of the poor Jews in these communities. Poverty limits even charitable giving. Together, climate, geographical access, money, and shortage of leisure time were constraining features in the expression of eastern European Judaism two centuries ago.

The picture is not much different when we consider formal Jewish education. Few persons were educated Jewishly two hundred years ago; there were few Jewish schools and no adequate Jewish curriculum, and the tutors or teachers were themselves poorly educated. If judged by partial and anecdotal evidence, these teachers were often more a discouragement to education than a stimulus to knowledge. (If truth be told, much of the Jewish education of a generation or two ago in the United States was seriously disheartening to thousands of American youngsters for much the same reason.) Most Jewish men and women at the beginning of the nineteenth century were illiterate in any language. Even if Jews could afford Jewish books, there were few to be purchased, and few people could have read them two hundred years ago. Jews were living in a Jewish cultural wasteland. At least in terms of synagogue attendance, Jewish education and the depth of Jewish literacy, and observance of some public and family religious rituals, Jews in the United States at the end of the twentieth century were doing much better than their forebears. Nevertheless, despite the information collected in our make-believe survey, only an incompetent social scientist would have concluded that Jews two centuries ago were not religious, that they did not "value" Jewish education, or that their communities were eroding.

Correctly, you might admonish me for presenting such superficial historical comparisons. The comparisons are distorting, you might say, because formal Jewish education, synagogue attendance, and ritual observances two centuries ago were limited by the resources available and by the absence of choice. In the home and within families, Jews were committed to their Judaism as much as circumstances permitted. They were Jewish by necessity if not always by choice, being responsive to the peer pressure of their Jewish friends and the discrimination of their non-Jewish neighbors.

These are powerful arguments, since they highlight the centrality of family and community in the development of Judaism and the quality of Jewish life in the home. Identical points can be made about contemporary American Judaism and Jewish education. American Jewish communities are not confronted with the same constraints of the past, but new constraints and newly emerging pressures operate in similar ways to limit exposure to Jewish education and the performance of some religious rituals. At the same time, new forms of communication and technologies bring Judaism from distant places to the homes of American Jews, even in remote areas of the country. And new Jewish rituals dot the American Jewish calendar as never before: Jewish craft fairs, observations of Israel Independence Day and Holocaust Memorial Day, scholar-in-residence weekends and special lectures on Jewish themes in universities, annual Jewish Federation meetings that draw organizations representing more than eight hundred localities and millions of Jews in the United States. Perhaps these replace some public religious rituals of the past. One need only look at the annual calendars of local Jewish communities around the United States to witness the enormous range of activities that characterizes them.

Being Jewish in the past was part of everyday life; it was the focal point of family and community. The major distinguishing feature of Judaism in the past was its connection to the totality of Jewish life, which means the association ties and the family-economic networks, the omnipresence of the Jewish community, the positive effects of being distinctive, the shared lifestyle and values. The totality of Jewish life in the past was intensive and cohesive, reinforcing the values and shared experiences of individuals.

I would argue that religious ritual observances, formal Jewish education, and attendance at religious services are no more and no less valid indicators of contemporary American Judaism than they were of Judaism two hundred years ago. Then, the work Jews did, the jobs they held, the institutions they created, and their cultural forms—the shared totality—reinforced a sense of distinctiveness and community among Jews. And non-Jews reminded them that they were a minority. So it is in the United States today. The numbers show that most Jews in the 1990s shared Jewish holidays and ritual occasions with other Jews (Passover, Hanukkah, and the High Holidays were the most popular). They shared commitments to the State of Israel and to charitable giving for Jewish causes. Most saw other Jews as their closest friends, many worked with other Jews, and many attended Jewish institutions and wanted to provide some Jewish education to their children—to transmit Jewish culture to the next generation. In general, Jews considered being Jewish one of the important things in their lives, even when it was as abstract as "tradition" and "family values." Indeed, for American Jews, being Jewish in some form is one of the most often expressed and deeply felt values. If poverty and lack of access to opportunities were the preoccupations of Jewish communities in the past, contemporary American Jews are distracted by their wealth and resources. The commonality of religious expression between the generations at the end of the twentieth century reinforces the bonds created in the home. Just as educational similarities between the generations are sources of family bonds and communal cohesion, the commonality of religious expression binds the generations. This is the case even when the religious basis of both generations is weak.

Unlike generations of several centuries ago, when Jews were raised in homes characterized by different levels of religious observance, and certainly unlike the immigrant generation and their children, the third and fourth generations of Jews in the United States have much in common culturally and in their religious attitudes. To be sure, their Judaism is secularized and transformed, but it is not a source of generational conflict. Among the younger generation, Judaism is not a stimulus for rejection and escape as it was in the past.

What is the content of contemporary American Jewish institutions? What makes them Jewish and not something else? Institutions selectively construct Jewish history and cultural memory. They provide one basis for cultural and religious continuity. This pattern is similar to that of families and generations of the past, who constructed their own versions of Jewish culture and religion even as the contents of their culture changed. It is the community, the networks, and the shared lifestyle, values, and concerns of American Jews that bind them together. The form and content of Jewishness are radically different today from those of the past. I argue that the community itself and the institutions that shape its culture are critical in terms of ethnic continuity. Institutions are the visible and conspicuous symbols of Jewish culture and the basis of Jewish communal activities.

In the contemporary United States, the evidence suggests that a critical part of Jewish continuity is connected to whether Jewish-based communal institutions exist. Jewish schools and libraries, Jewish homes for the aged, Jewish community centers, and many and diverse temples and synagogues are important elements in the development of American communities. These institutions compete with one another for loyalty and commitments. Playing golf together with other Jews in a mostly Jewish country club, swimming and playing softball at the Jewish community center, or using day-care facilities in a Jewish institutional setting do not seem, on the surface, to be very Jewish, but they are. They are part of that total round of activity that makes for a community of intertwined networks.

These "secular" activities within Jewish institutions can enhance the values of Jewish life, intensify shared commitments, and broaden the social, family, and economic networks that sustain the continuity of the Jewish community. They may also reinforce the value of Jewish religious rituals and religious institutional activities. Using Jewish institutions to create networks sets up the potential for improving the quality of Jewish life and ensuring its continuity. All of these activities together, not only the formal educational ones and not only the religious ritual ones, form what I mean by community. Indeed, studies show that the "secular" activities of Jewish life reinforce the "religious," and vice versa, because so many Jews participate in them. The intensities often go together because they lead to the same place—the Jewish community. And it is community that shapes the lives and future of Jews in the United States, as it did in the past. The connection between the family and these communal institutions therefore becomes a central feature of Jewish continuity.

But haven't the religious changes resulted in secularization? Let us

undertake another mental exercise, one that carries us back even far-
ther in time. Imagine a time a generation after the destruction of the
temple in Jerusalem, when no animal sacrifices are being brought there.
Some rabbis begin to argue that prayer can substitute for animal
sacrifices. Other rabbis no doubt argue that the prayer substitute is not
only changing but diminishing Judaism. Certainly the sociologists of
the era (had there been any by that name), measuring the Jews' changing ritual practices, recognize that measures of ritual dating from the
days of animal sacrifice no longer reveal the nature of religious activity.
The priests, the *kohanim,* are concerned about the decline of Jewish ritual activities, as they understand them. Many suggest that the new generation is moving away from Judaism. Some social scientist researchers
of the time, however, are arguing about transformation, not decline. These
researchers (some refer to them as the rabbis of the Talmud) are replac-
ing sacrifice with prayer and the priests with rabbis. The transforming
experience of a Judaism that is not based on animal sacrifice is probably rejected by many. Some historians argue that things have changed
and the end of the Jewish people is occurring. Or at least, there appears
to be a decline in religiosity, judging from what had been understood
in the past. "Return us to the days of our glory, when we can again bring
animal sacrifices in the temple," some proclaim, making this plea a part
of their daily prayers. In our longer view, and in retrospect, it is clear
that the transformation away from animal sacrifice probably saved
Judaism from certain demise.

EUROPE AND ISRAEL

I have focused in this chapter on the transformation of Jews in the United
States, the development of their institutions, and the remarkable choices
they have made about their Jewishness and Judaism. This is not to argue
that there have been no declines in some aspects of American Jewish
communal life; there clearly have been. But taking the broader perspective, I have suggested that Jewish communities in the United States
have developed new and creative forms of Jewish culture. I do not define
change as decline, or the development of new forms of Jewish culture
and religion as secularization. Rather, I argue for a more dynamic view

of change that implies the value of choice, diversity, and creativity in the emergence of new forms. Some social scientists have missed these new forms by measuring only older forms, and some have dismissed them as the last gasps of a dying community. I reject both points of view and argue that Jewish cultural forms are emergent and developing and are likely to serve as the new basis of American Jewish communities in coming generations.

What about Judaism and Jewish culture in Israel? And what are the signs of Jewish cultural change among European Jewish communities? Do they show the same patterns as those in the United States? If Judaism were only personal and individual, then Israeli Jews would be facing a similar crisis, because they, too, are predominantly secular. But the strength of Israeli Jews and their communities lies not in their Judaism. Indeed, religion is enormously divisive in Israel. Instead, Israel's strength lies in the institutions it has created and in its everyday life. The State of Israel is a strong Jewish community because of the interaction among its Jews socially, culturally, and politically and because of the significant role of families there. Collective nationalism and culture sustain families when religion is weak and divisive. Extensive interaction almost totally among Jews in jobs, schools, neighborhoods, and the military is the basis for Jewish cohesion in Israel. Even without the country's external constraints (threats of war and perceptions of conflict and siege), there are strong bases of cohesion among its Jews.

The divisiveness of religion in Israel may be linked to its politics and patronage systems. There has been no religious renaissance of any magnitude in Israeli Judaism. Moderate forms of religion (whether liberal or the conservative Masorti movement) have not developed among the younger generation. Israeli Judaism manifests itself largely in the reactionary elements of *haredi*, or ultra-Orthodox, Judaism in it various forms and in the role of religious political parties among Sephardic Jews. Unlike in communities outside of Israel, where religion marks off Jews from non-Jews, inside Israel Judaism tends to divide Jews. There is increasing anti-religious feeling among the majority of the secular Israeli Jewish public. Religious and secular Jews are separated residentially and institutionally, and extreme geographical concentration characterizes the ultra-Orthodox. The more institutionally religious Israeli Jews are powerfully articulate about government policies regarding religion, and the settler population in the Palestinian areas administered by Israel is politically outspoken as well.

A 1999–2000 poll in Israel revealed some important characteristics of religious identity and religiosity among Jewish Israelis.[10] At that time, a minority of Israeli Jews defined themselves as religious (17 percent reported that they were *dati* [religious] and/or *haredi*), 43 percent defined themselves as nonreligious, and 5 percent described themselves as anti-religious. About one-third defined themselves as "traditional" (Masorti), a decline from the 42 percent who identified themselves that way in an earlier survey in 1991. Consistent with the way people categorized themselves, only a minority of respondents (16 percent) report that they are careful about observing the tradition, 20 percent report that they generally observe, 43 percent say they partially observe, and 21 percent do not observe at all.

The most accepted Jewish ritual in Israel, according to the 1999–2000 survey, is the use of the mezuzah (98 percent of respondents reported using it), followed by holding a Passover seder (85 percent) and lighting Hanukkah candles (71 percent). These are public displays of Jewishness, as well as family-related activities. Only a small proportion of the Jewish Israeli population (15 percent) prays daily in a synagogue or wears a head covering. Large proportions of Jews fast on Yom Kippur (67 percent) and observe dietary regulations by eating only kosher foods (58 percent). The proportion eating nonkosher foods has increased significantly over the decade between the two surveys, from 16 percent to 42 percent, and seder participation has increased slightly. In 1999–2000, about half the Israeli Jewish population reported that relationships between ethnic groups in Israel were poor (up from 33 percent a decade earlier); 82 percent said that the religious-secular relationship was poor (72 percent reported so in 1990). About seven out of ten reported that Jews in Israel and in the Diaspora were two different peoples (compared with 57 percent in 1990), and 30 percent believed that Jews in Israel and in the Diaspora did not have a joint destiny (up from 24 percent in 1991). These data lead to three important conclusions: Jews in Israel have moved in the direction of greater secularism while differences between religious and secular have widened; Jews in

Israel think that ethnic divisions have increased; and Jews in Israel are not particularly "religious," even if they are inescapably Jewish.

Israeli Jews of Middle Eastern origins, the so-called Mizrahim, report that they are much more religious and observant than those of Western origins, the Ashkenazim. A large majority of the nonreligious Jews are Ashkenazim, and the ultra-Orthodox sector is also largely Ashkenazi. Most Mizrahim define themselves as "traditional" (compared with 19 percent of the Ashkenazim); few are nonreligious or anti-religious (9 percent of the Mizrahim versus 34 percent of the Ashkenazim).

Many aspects of Israeli social life bind Jewish Israelis to one another, and external factors during and between crises reinforce these ties. At the same time, and in interesting ways, Israelis lump ethnic origins into the broad geographical categories "European-American" and "Asian-African." These categories have become divisive, in large part because they reflect primarily social inequalities rather than culturally neutral differences. The overlap of social class and regional residential clusters is not a simple carryover from places and cultures of origin; divisions are often Israeli created.[11] Distinctions between Jews of Western and Middle Eastern origins extend to the second generation, and there are firm grounds for predicting the continuation of these ethnic divisions for at least another generation.

What are the prospects for Jewish cultural renewal in Europe? European Jewish communities are embedded in larger, well-established national units. They have rich institutional traditions and more direct memories of the Holocaust. Unlike American Jews, most European Jews are centrally organized. Through migration and related processes, they have become more diverse in the last several decades. As a result, their rich legacies from the past are unlikely to be a guide to their future. Traditional measures of religion and religious ritual observances will not show stability, much less increases, in secular Europe. New forms of commitment to Jewishness, however—often reinforced by the continuation of some forms of anti-Semitism—seem likely to ensure some ethnic consciousness in the younger generation. The migration of a significant number of Muslims to major European centers is likely to reinforce Jewish cultural distinctiveness. Migration, competitive new institutions, anti-Semitism, and memories of the Holocaust remain the characteristics of most European communities. Negative demographic trends, which apply to European populations as a whole, are unlikely to imply the end of European Jewry. There has been no discernible religious revival in Europe or among European Jews, and a broad, secular Jewish cultural renaissance is more likely.

I mainly have questions regarding the future of institutions and networks among European Jewry. Will the Jews of post-Holocaust Europe and the former Soviet Union develop Jewish institutions to generate new forms of Jewish culture? There are early signs of Jewish renewal in Russia, as there are in France and Britain. Such renewal is less likely to take place in the longer-established, centralized Jewish religious institutions and organizations. Both secularization and new forms of Jewish culture require new institutional bases.

Recent historical reviews of the Jewish communities in France and the former Soviet Union reinforce the power and importance of new institutional dimensions of Jewish life.[12] In both communities, migration has played a critical role in reshaping the ethnic and religious cultural blend and the community's connections to other communities around the world, particularly in the United States and Israel. The immigration of North African Jews to France and of Soviet Jews to places west and to Israel has challenged the continuity of these Jewish communities. The recent reviews provide a basis for a positive assessment of the future of these communities that is based on a combination of emergent Jewish values in specific national contexts. Most importantly, these evaluations in no way correspond to the doom and gloom of the demographic projections or the assertion that the European communities are part of the vanishing Diaspora.

How might Jewish institutions reinforce Jewish cohesion? By establishing Jewish institutions—gathering places for learning, study, prayer, and cultural and social activities—Jews reaffirm their distinctiveness not simply as individuals, not only as families, but also as a community. Individuals die, families are formed and re-formed, but institutions can have continuity over many generations, far beyond the lives of the people who established them. Jews are distinctive as a community because their institutions are distinctive. The communities that have flourished are those in which institutions have change built into their structure. Institutions create the basis of communal solidarity.

People construct their communities, families, and friends around institutions (even the kinds of institutions established reflect communities' values). Their prayers come together in public places, as do their collective goals, communal bonds, and commitments to survive as a community. Only those ethnic and religious groups that develop institutions survive in the melting pot called society. In large part that is because institutions remind people who they are in history and in culture and inform their neighbors who they are as well. Such institutions are surely constructed in different ways now than in the past, but they serve the same goals of community and distinctiveness.

Jews create institutions—federations, Hillels (Jewish student campus organizations), synagogues and temples, schools, community centers, museums and Holocaust foundations, philanthropies, welfare and other local organizations. They invest in them, expand them, serve on their boards. The institutions provide major benefits to the community as a whole. From the point of view of organizational goals, they define the nature of Jewish culture, Jewish creativity, and Jewish continuity. The old joke about the lone shipwrecked Jew who built two synagogues, one that he attended and one that he didn't, symbolizes the enormous capacity of Jews to build institutional Jewish life even while joking about it among themselves.

SOME CONCLUDING THOUGHTS

With this new orientation toward the past in mind, let us revisit the themes we need to reckon with in order to understand contemporary Jewish communities and their futures. Defining who is included in Jewish communities is not simply a research question for social scientists but a profound theoretical and practical concern. In a voluntary community, people define themselves in and out of the community at various points in their lives. One consequence is that researchers who take snapshots of the community at the moment of a single survey, and not dynamic moving pictures, obtain distorted images of ethnic identity and community. Life course transitions, such as periods when young adults are no longer living at home but have not yet started families of their own, are particularly vulnerable. People's ethnic and religious identity is often in flux at such moments, and their communal commitments throughout the remainder of the life course are difficult to forecast.

Categorizing some Jews as "core" and others as "peripheral," as was done in the formal reports of the U.S. National Jewish Population Survey in 1990, is to do more than establish an arbitrary classification system. The distinction is a polarizing social construction of the margins of the community, designed to justify policy initiatives directed at the core and not at the periphery. Rabbi Jonathan Sachs, the chief rabbi of Great Britain, calls this "Jewish Darwinism"—only the fittest Jews survive, and therefore only they are deserving of support and policy attention. And the categorization itself is based on a cross-sectional snapshot obtained by asking questions over the telephone about current Jewish identification.

While family values and cohesion are central to the understanding of contemporary Jewish communities, few sociological studies have had a family focus. We sociologists have been primarily concerned with individual identity. When we focus on family, we tend to measure only group processes of fertility and family structure, yet we have argued theoretically for the power of networks as a basis for continuity among ethnic populations. We need to refocus on the future of family networks. The American Jewish community's obsession with marriage and intermarriage has not led to studies of children and young adults who are not living at home. We argue about generational continuities, the core of communal changes, but we do not study life course transitions.

How do we conceptualize the Jewish family? Too often we start (and end) with indicators of family deterioration. We need to study how Jewish families strengthen their communities. We need to begin systematic studies not only of couples but also of blended families, reconstituted families, intermarried families, stepfamilies, and their children. And when we study families, we need to look beyond the nuclear family to identify the roles of extended relatives and kin. Incorporating the gender emphasis in our research requires us at a minimum to examine relationships between men and women and between parents and children.

The gender switch in Jewish intermarriages, in which increasing numbers of Jewish women are marrying non-Jews, may be of particular importance in Jewish continuity. These family patterns in turn need to be related to institutional structures, synagogues, and Jewish organizations and to be linked to what is happening in Jewish homes.

How do we take religious transformation into account? Sociologists have incorporated in their surveys, and appropriately so, measures of the intensity of religious expression. Which Jewish surveys since the 1960s have not included questions about candle lighting on Friday night or at Hanukkah, or about Passover seder celebrations? On the basis of responses to such questions, they have concluded something about changes and variations in the religious activities of Jews. They have also concluded something about religious decline and secularization. However, if we had only these survey questionnaires as guides to what Judaism is, we would have a most distorted view. If the survey questionnaire were our Judaic text, we would conclude that some religious rituals are more important than others. Is candle lighting more important to measure than people's having a Friday night dinner with family members, visiting the sick, or doing other good deeds? The rabbis of the Talmud could not prioritize among the mitzvot, the commandments and charitable acts; how arrogant of social scientists to do so. How distorting to assert that we understand contemporary Judaism by examining the results of our past national surveys. Have we biased our views of those "Jews on the periphery" by measuring whether they attend synagogue regularly or how often they fast on Yom Kippur? Do we dismiss their seders and Hanukkah celebrations by noting that they are "only" occasions for family get-togethers and that Hanukkah is "only" the Jewish counterpoint to Christmas in the United States?

Where are the institutions in our research? If networks are missing entirely, where do we put Jewish institutions? Of course we have included in our surveys questions about whether people are synagogue members or give charitable contributions to the Jewish federations, but do we ask whether living in a place that has a Jewish community center or a Jewish day-care center or a home for the aged matters for the quality of Jewish life? Do we find out in our surveys whether Jewish day care strengthens Jewish networks and communities? Does our emphasis on national Jewish studies mask the rich diversity among Jewish communities?

Finally, we need to evaluate Jewish education, not just to study how many years and in what types of institutions people obtain their education. I have often argued that the quality of a university course is measured by how much the instructor learns. I would similarly argue that the quality of Jewish education, especially at the younger ages, is measured by how much the parents learn. As far as I know, we have never obtained systematic information about these aspects of education in our demographic and community surveys.

The key and most powerful finding of sociologists' research is the importance of examining the quality of Jewish life. Clearly there is an interaction between the numbers and the quality—indeed, one needs a minyan for some purposes, but who is counted toward that quorum is not a social science question on which "hard data" can shed light.

Two critical points about futures need to be stressed. One is the diversity of Jewish communities. This means that what works for one community may not work for others. The diversity proposition is important within the United States and between the United States and other countries. If my premise that contexts count is correct (social, political, cultural, and economic contexts, plus institutional and historical contexts), then it follows that when context changes, Judaism changes. When contexts vary, Jewishness and Judaism vary as well. The expectation is that community variation is normal, not exceptional. Hence we should not be surprised that measures of what characterizes the community in various places should vary. We are unlikely to consider the extent of monthly *mikvah* use as an indicator of Jewish identity in the twenty-first century, nor would finding out about the wearing of clothing made of wool and linen *(shatnez)* be useful. We might have used these indicators in nineteenth-century Morocco or in the eastern European shtetl Slobodka. We would not use only the public celebrations of Hanukkah and Rosh Hashanah as indicators of how communities in the 1950s expressed their Judaism.

We have entered a new century and a new millennium. Continuity with the past is limited when the communities we are studying have changed so drastically. We should be focusing on community. We should be focusing on families. Why are we diverting our energies from these grand questions about Judaism and the Jewishness to obsess about biology? Imagine what would happen if 90 percent of American Jews were ending up with marriage partners who happened to have been born Jews but cared little about their Jewishness. There would likely be no perceived crisis, and we would not be concerned about Jewish continuity in the United States. There would be no perceived erosion, no perceived demographic decline, and we probably would not be arguing among ourselves about the right ways to investigate the decline of Judaism.

Whatever the message the American Jewish community thinks it is sending to the next generation, most of them hear the following:

> We Jews are great musicians. Your grandparents were musicians, as were their parents before them. For centuries our people have made the most extraordinary music. Therefore the number one priority of our community is that whomever you marry should have a mother who is a musician.
>
> These young people are smart and perplexed by this message. "We don't get it," they might say. "There was relatively little music in our homes when we were growing up. A couple of times a year we went to big concerts where we didn't know the score. We enjoy hearing the music from time to time even though we can barely read a note. If music is so important to our family and to our community, why is it that the only thing I hear them talking about is whether or not my potential mother-in-law is a musician?"[13]

Jewish families and institutions, Jewish homes and communities have been the music of Jewish lives. I hope that Jews and their children and their partners, and their children's children and their partners, will learn to play this music and contribute to this great unfolding Jewish symphony.

NOTES

I / STUDYING THE JEWISH FUTURE

1. W. Warren Wagar, *A History of the Future* (Chicago: University of Chicago Press, 1999). See also the afterword by I. Wallerstein in that volume.

2. See Calvin Goldscheider and Alan Zuckerman, *The Transformation of the Jews* (Chicago: University of Chicago Press, 1984). Among others, see the studies in Jonathan Webber, ed., *Jewish Identities in the New Europe* (London: Littman Library of Jewish Civilization, 1994); Todd Endelman, ed., *Comparing Jewish Societies* (Ann Arbor: University of Michigan Press, 1997); and Pierre Birnbaum and Ira Katznelson, eds., *Paths of Emancipation: Jews, States, and Citizenship* (Princeton, N.J.: Princeton University Press, 1995).

3. See Arland Thornton, "The Development Paradigm, Reading History Sideways, and Family Change," *Demography* 38, no. 4 (November 2001): 449–65.

4. On historians' rejection of the lachrymose conception of Jewish history, see the note by Yosef Hayim Yerushalmi in his classic book *Zakhor: Jewish History and Jewish Memory* (Seattle: University of Washington Press, 1996), 132.

5. See Louis Finkelstein, ed., *The Jews: Their History, Culture, and Religion* (New York: Harper, 1949), and Marshall Sklare, ed., *The Jews: Social Patterns of an American Group* (New York: Free Press, 1958).

2 / THE FUTURES OF JEWISH COMMUNITIES IN THE UNITED STATES, EUROPE, AND ISRAEL

1. Norman Cantor, *The Sacred Chain: The History of the Jews* (New York: HarperCollins, 1994), 426, 434, 437.

2. Charles Krauthammer, "At Last, Zion: Israel and the Fate of the Jews," *The Weekly Standard*, 11 May 1998, 25.

3. Sergio DellaPergola, *World Jewry beyond 2000: The Demographic Prospects*, Occasional Papers no. 2, Third Frank Green Lecture (Oxford: Oxford Centre for Hebrew and Jewish Studies, 1999).

4. The category containing those born non-Jews who are married to born Jews encompasses a great deal of variability. At the most elementary level, it is necessary to differentiate non-Jewish-born spouses who have converted to Judaism from those who have not converted. I am not concerned here about the halachic issues of conversion, nor am I focusing on the auspices of religious conversions; instead, I am focusing on the social definitions of belonging to the Jewish community. Substantial numbers of spouses convert under the auspices of Orthodox, Conservative, and Reform Judaism, with their various criteria. No less important are non-Jewish spouses who have not formally converted but who are Jewishly identified and likely to be raising Jewish children. Those who have formally converted to Judaism are generally more likely to be committed to raising the next generation as Jewish. They also tend to be more religiously committed than the unconverted and more closely identified with Jewish communal activities. Little research has been done on the relative intensity of observances of the converted by religious denomination. Since American Jews in general tend not to be religiously observant, it has generally been found that the converted are no less observant than the Jewish born. The critical issue, about which there is little evidence but considerable speculation, is the Jewishness of the household in which one family member was not born Jewish. For methodological and research reasons, no systematic evidence exists on the Jewishness of those raised in families in which one parent was born non-Jewish at the point in the life cycle where the offspring form families of their own.

5. Simon Rawidowicz, *Israel: The Ever-Dying People and Other Essays*, edited by Benjamin Ravid (Cranbury, N.J.: Associated University Presses, 1986).

6. See the discussion in Lynn Davidman and Shelly Tenenbaum, eds., *Feminist Perspectives on Jewish Studies* (New Haven, Conn.: Yale University Press, 1994).

7. This is the title of Bernard Wasserstein's book *Vanishing Diaspora: The Jews in Europe since 1945* (Cambridge, Mass.: Harvard University Press, 1996). A similar title on American Jews in a popular version is *The Vanishing American Jew* by Alan Dershowitz (New York: Little, Brown, 1997).

8. Jonathan Webber, ed., *Jewish Identities in the New Europe* (London: Littman Library of Jewish Civilization, 1994), ix.

9. David Vital, *The Future of the Jews* (Cambridge, Mass.: Harvard University Press, 1990), 104, 105, 107.

10. Wasserstein, *Vanishing Diaspora,* 280, 284, 290.

11. Sergio DellaPergola and Uzi Rebhun, "Projecting a Rare Population: World Jews 2000–2080" (paper presented at the annual meeting of the Population Association of America, March 2001).

12. Webber, *Jewish Identities,* 26–27.

13. Wasserstein, *Vanishing Diaspora.*

14. On Israel's changing population and its implications for the future, see Calvin Goldscheider, *Israel's Changing Society,* second edition (Boulder, Colo.: Westview Press, 2002).

15. Ibid.

3 / FORECASTING JEWISH POPULATIONS

1. There are abundant technical sources that may be consulted on the calculations and limitations of demographic forecasting. See, for example, John Bongaarts and Rodolfo Bulatao, eds., *Beyond Six Billion: Forecasting the World's Population* (Washington, D.C.: National Academy Press, 2000), and Wolfgang Lutz, James Vaupel, and Dennis Ahlburg, eds., *Frontiers of Population Forecasting* (*Population and Development Review,* supplement, vol. 24, 1998). The most comprehensive set of critiques of population forecasts for its time—and the most fun to read—can be found in Pitirim Sorokin, *Fads and Foibles in Modern Sociology* (Chicago: Henry Regnery, 1956), particularly chapters 7, 8, and 11. For an early assessment, see J. J. Spengler, "Population Predictions in Nineteenth-Century America," *American Sociological Review* 1, no. 6 (December 1936): 905–21.

2. See DellaPergola and Rebhun, "Projecting a Rare Population." All quotations in this and subsequent sections are from this paper, unless otherwise specified. The paper contains a substantial bibliography, including references to many other population projections by the senior author and his colleagues at the Institute of Contemporary Jewry of the Hebrew University of Jerusalem. These projections are continuous with those prepared over the last several decades by DellaPergola's mentors, Roberto Bachi and Oscar Schmelz. The importance of these projections is that they represent several generations of thinking about

population futures and have been institutionalized within the Institute of
Contemporary Jewry. They have also been influential in the articulation of population and communal policies in Israel and the United States. For projections
that focus on the Jewish population in the United States, assuming continuous,
unchanging demographic rates, see Vivian Klaff, "Broken Down by Age and Sex:
Projecting the Jewish Population," *Contemporary Jewry* 19 (1998): 1–37.

3. By "current" fertility, demographers mean the distribution of births (or number of children) by age of the mother (the cross section) in a given year. These
are the number of children born in a given year (not the total number of children ever born to women over their life course). The assumption is that the births
to women at the older ages of a given year represent the future childbearing of
women in the younger ages and the births to younger women represent the past
childbearing of the older women. Hence the distribution of births is a cross section of the population (in a given year) and not necessarily the actual total number of children that they will have. Any change in the timing of childbearing,
in the timing of marriage or union formation, or in the distribution of births
by age will influence estimates of completed family size based on the current
cross section. Thus, if older women are having more children now than in the
past, and younger women are having fewer children, the fertility estimates by
age in the cross section will be distorting. Fertility estimates for constructing
population projections for Israel and for Diaspora Jewish populations are based
only on current patterns of childbearing. The evidence indicates, however, that
current fertility rates are less revealing of completed family size than they are
of delayed marriage and childbearing in the United States.

4. The estimated average family size of 2.1 in the United States in 2002 is
the highest this figure has been in thirty years. It places the United States at the
high end of fertility in developed nations, with Britain now at 1.7 and Australia
at 1.8. How the Jewish community fits into these new fertility data is unknown.
But changes (even increases) in fertility have to be built into projections for the
future. Press release from the United States National Center for Health Statistics,
February 13, 2002.

5. See Calvin Goldscheider and Frances Goldscheider, "Family Size Expectations of Young American Jewish Adults," in O. Schmelz and S. DellaPergola,
eds., *Papers in Jewish Demography: 1985* (Institute of Contemporary Jewry,
1989).

6. DellaPergola, *World Jewry beyond 2000,* 42.

7. Bruce Philips, "The Vanishing American Jew: The Cultural Dynamics Perspective," paper presented at the annual meeting of the Association for Jewish Studies, Boston, December 2000.

8. See my discussion and Table 1 in chapter 2.

9. See Calvin Goldscheider, *Cultures in Conflict: The Arab-Israeli Conflict* (Westport, Conn.: Greenwood, 2002), and Goldscheider, *Israel's Changing Society*.

10. See William Petersen, *Population* (New York: Macmillan, 1969), 333; see also Bongaarts and Bulatao, *Beyond Six Billion: Forcasting the World's Population*, 15 n.1, for the distinctions between forecasting and projections. Among other things, a forecast is a predictive distribution of possible future outcomes.

11. Bongaarts and Bulatao, *Beyond Six Billion*, 189–90.

12. Jane Menken, "Preface," in Bongaarts and Bulatao, *Beyond Six Billion*. See also the discussion in chapter 7 of the same book.

13. This is the basis of the synthetic life table measurement of mortality and was the fundamental assumption in fertility projections that led to the most embarrassing demographic errors of projection in the 1930s and 1940s.

14. Bongaarts and Bulatao, *Beyond Six Billion*, 83, 106.

15. Frances Goldscheider and Linda Waite, *New Families, No Families?: The Transformation of the American Home* (Berkeley: University of California Press, 1991).

16. Bongaarts and Bulatao, *Beyond Six Billion*, 73.

17. Calvin Goldscheider, *Population, Modernization, and Social Structure* (New York: Little Brown, 1971).

18. See Ronald Freedman, Pascal Whelpton, and Arthur Campbell, *Family Planning, Fertility, and Population Growth* (New York: McGraw Hill, 1959).

19. See Frances Goldscheider and Calvin Goldscheider, *Leaving Home before Marriage* (Madison: University of Wisconsin Press, 1993).

20. For an assessment of how censuses treat ethnic groups over time, and of changing ethnic definitions in the United States, Canada, and Israel, see Calvin Goldscheider, "Ethnic Categorizations in Censuses: Comparative Observations from Israel, Canada, and the United States," in David Kertzer and Dominique Arel, eds., *Census and Identity: The Politics of Race, Ethnicity, and Language in National Censuses* (Cambridge: Cambridge University Press, 2002).

21. For a review of conditions in these areas, see Goldscheider and Zuckerman, *Transformation of the Jews*, chapter 2.

22. Arthur Ruppin was a colleague of Roberto Bachi, the founder of the demography unit of the Institute of Contemporary Jewry at the Hebrew University of Jerusalem. Both were teachers and mentors of Oscar Schmelz. Sergio DellaPergola was a student of Bachi's and Schmelz's and has been director of the Institute of Contemporary Jewry and head of its demography unit. He is currently a professor of Jewish demography and statistics at the Hebrew University of Jerusalem. DellaPergola and his student Uzi Rehbun prepared the projections noted earlier. See also Sergio DellaPergola, "Arthur Ruppin Revisited: The Jews of Today, 1904–1994," in Steven M. Cohen and Gabriel Horencyzk, eds., *National Variations in Jewish Identity: Implications for Jewish Education* (Albany: State University of New York Press, 1999).

23. See the details in Dov Friedlander and Calvin Goldscheider, "Peace and the Future Demography of Israel," *Journal of Conflict Resolution* 18 (September 1974): 486–501.

4 / THE CENTRALITY OF JEWISH VALUES
IN SHAPING THE JEWISH FUTURE

1. The review of Shmuel's life is based on an unpublished manuscript I wrote jointly with the well-known translator, author, and writer Jeffrey Green. Together, we formally interviewed Shmuel Braw and transcribed and edited these interviews about his life. What follows are small selections and edited excerpts from that manuscript, with a focus on futures and Jewish values. In addition to the hours we spent formally interviewing Shmuel—and being interviewed by him—in my home in Jerusalem, I spent hundreds of hours in the 1970s and 1980s informally talking to him and his family in the synagogue in Talpiot, Jerusalem, in their home in Jerusalem, in Kiryat Gat, and in Kibbutz Ein Tzurim.

2. This was published in Goldscheider and Zuckerman, *Transformation of the Jews*.

5 / WHAT PROPHECY AND ANIMAL SACRIFICES REVEAL
ABOUT CONTEMPORARY JEWISH COMMUNITIES

1. The rabbis in the Talmud list forty-eight male prophets and seven female prophets (Megillah 14A). Contrary to the passage in Deuteronomy, some non-

Jews are defined as prophets elsewhere in the Torah and in the Talmud; the best known was Balaam, as noted in Numbers 22–24.

2. Ernie Frerichs brought to my attention the verse from 1 Samuel 9:9, which says that "he who is now called a prophet was formerly called a seer." It seems to me that the seer is a futurist and that the rabbis of the Talmud rejected that element of the prophet's voice.

3. I take this insight from Elliot Dorff and Arthur Rosett, *A Living Tree: The Roots and Growth of Jewish Law* (Albany: State University of New York Press, 1988).

4. Indeed, Jacob Neusner has argued that the focus of the midrash on Leviticus (Leviticus Rabbah) is upon the society of Israel, its national fate and moral condition. The text of Leviticus that deals with the holy temple is interpreted in the context of the holy people Israel. See J. Neusner, *Invitation to Midrash: The Working of Rabbinic Interpretation* (New York: Harper and Row, 1989).

5. I am not sure this tribute can be defined, in contemporary terms, as the vegetarian's or animal rights supporter's substitute sacrifice. But that there was a substitute for the poor suggests an important flexibility about contribution, as well as a respect for diversity that could be translated into respect for those who have different views of animal rights and are against the consumption of animal products.

6 / SECULARISM, RELIGION, ETHNICITY, AND ASSIMILATION

1. See the evidence in Goldscheider, *Israel's Changing Society.*

2. See Jonathan Woocher, *Sacred Survival: The Civil Religion of American Jews* (Bloomington: Indiana University Press, 1986).

3. For an overview, see, among others, Gerald Gorin, *A Time for Building: The Third Migration 1880–1920* (Baltimore, Md.: Johns Hopkins University Press, 1992); and Goldscheider and Zuckerman, *Transformation of the Jews.*

4. See Simon Kuznets, "Economic Structure and Life of the Jews," in L. Finkelstein, ed., *The Jews* (Philadelphia: Jewish Publication Society, 1960), 1597–1666; Stanley Lieberson, *A Piece of the Pie: Blacks and White Immigrants since 1880* (Berkeley: University of California Press, 1980); and Goldscheider and Zuckerman, *Transformation of the Jews.*

5. Joel Perlmann, *Ethnic Differences: Schooling and Social Structure among the Irish, Italians, Jews, and Blacks in an American City, 1880–1935* (Cambridge:

Cambridge University Press, 1988); Stephen Steinberg, *The Academic Melting Pot* (New York: Carnegie Foundation, 1974).

6. For the empirical details, see Calvin Goldscheider, "Stratification and the Transformation of American Jews, 1910–1990: Have the Changes Resulted in Assimilation?" *Papers in Jewish Demography, Jewish Population Studies* (The Hebrew University of Jerusalem) 27 (1997): 259–76.

7. See, for example, Barry Chiswick, "Jewish Immigrant Skill and Occupational Attainment at the Turn of the Century," *Explorations in Economic History* 28 (1991): 64–86; Thomas Kessner, *The Golden Door: Italian and Jewish Immigrant Mobility in New York City, 1880–1915* (New York: Oxford University Press, 1977); Lieberson, *A Piece of the Pie;* and Calvin Goldscheider, *Jewish Continuity and Change* (Bloomington: Indiana University Press, 1986).

8. The following data are from Esther Wilder, "Socioeconomic Attainment and Expressions of Jewish Identification: 1970 and 1990," *Journal for the Scientific Study of Religion* 35, no. 2 (1996): 109–27. The interpretations are mine.

9. Wilder, "Socioeconomic Attainment."

10. This poll was reported in *Ha'aretz,* a Hebrew-language daily newspaper in Israel, March 27, 2002, pp. 1 and 10a, and in Shlomit Levy, Hanna Levinsohn, and Elihu Katz, *A Portrait of Israeli Jews: Beliefs, Observances, and Values among Israeli Jews, 2000* (Jerusalem: Israel Democracy Institute and Avi Chai Institute, 2002).

11. See the evidence in Goldscheider, *Israel's Changing Society.*

12. See in particular the thoughtful and authoritative historical account of the Jewish community of modern France in Paula Hyman, *The Jews of Modern France* (Berkeley: University of California Press, 1998). On Jewish life in the former Soviet Union, see Zvi Gitelman, "The Future of Jewish Life in the Former Soviet Union: Some Scenarios," background paper commissioned by the Memorial Foundation for Jewish Culture, Executive Committee meeting, Moscow, July 2001.

13. This passage is quoted from an insightful piece by Michael Brooks in *Sh'ma,* October 1999.

INDEX

Tarnow, 74–83
Tel Aviv, 43
Thailand, 43
Torah, 87–91, 95–99
Torat Kohanim, 93

Ukraine, 79
ultra-Orthodox, 131
United States, 74, 93, 100–104.
    See also America
universalism, 7
Uzbekistan, 79

values, Jewish, 5–8, 16, 19, 72–73,
    83–84, 95–99, 102–4. *See also*
    Jewish culture; Jewishness;
    Judaism

Vayikra Rabbah, 94
Vital, David, 35

Wagar, Warren, 3, 4
Wasserstein, Bernard, 41–42
West Bank, 55, 70

Yad Vashem, 76
Yeshiva, 14
Yiddish, 73, 74, 75, 83, 111–13
yiddishkeit, 42, 81, 83
Yom Kippur, 130

Zecharia, 90
Zionism, 6, 7; as ethnic nationalism,
    7
Zionist, 6, 15, 35, 39, 67, 72, 76, 80, 81